BEST PUB WALKS
in & around
SHEFFIELD

Clive Price

Published by Sigma Leisure – an imprint of
Sigma Press, 1 South Oak Lane, Wilmslow, Cheshire SK9 6AR, England.

British Library Cataloguing in Publication Data
A CIP record for this book is available from the British Library.

ISBN: 1-85058-435-4

Typesetting and Design by: Sigma Press, Wilmslow, Cheshire.

Printed by: MFP Design & Print

Cover photograph: The Crown Inn, Totley (Chris Rushton)

Maps: Jeremy Semmens

Photographs: the author

Acknowledgments: In the preparation of this volume of walks I have received prompt and courteous replies to my queries from the Rev. Roger Smith, Rector of Barnborough, Alison Cooper, Pat Clark, Helen Purves and Miss S. Linton of the Sheffield Libraries and Information Services, Anthony P. Munford, Archivist with the Department of Libraries, Museum and Arts of Rotherham Metropolitan Borough Council and the staff of Doncaster Metropolitan Borough Council Libraries Service. I am also indebted to Dean A. Jones, Information Officer for the South Yorkshire Passenger Transport Executive for details of bus services and Peter J. Gross, Marketing Manager for South Yorkshire Supertram Limited.

Contents

The Walks

Walk 25. High Melton   139

Climb to one of the most attractive villages in South Yorkshire before
crossing a prairie to a gruesome spot and returning by a holy well.

Distance: 6 miles.

Walk 26. Clayton   146

Walk from an old mining village across open countryside to an ancient
and attractive village of sandstone houses.

Distance: 5 miles.

Walk 27. Swinton   151

A short easy walk using woodland and field paths through gentle
countryside which has some points of historical interest.

Distance: 3 miles.

Walk 28. Wentworth   156

Explore the heart of the Wentworth Woodhouse estate. Pass through
parkland and see the largest private residence in England.

Distance: 6 miles.

Walk 29. Elsecar   163

A rural oasis in the heart of the South Yorkshire coalfield. Field paths and
bridleways traverse a rolling landscape.

Distance: 3½ miles.

Walk 30. Jump   168

A short route through a former mining area using field paths, roads and a
canal towpath.

Distance: 4 miles.

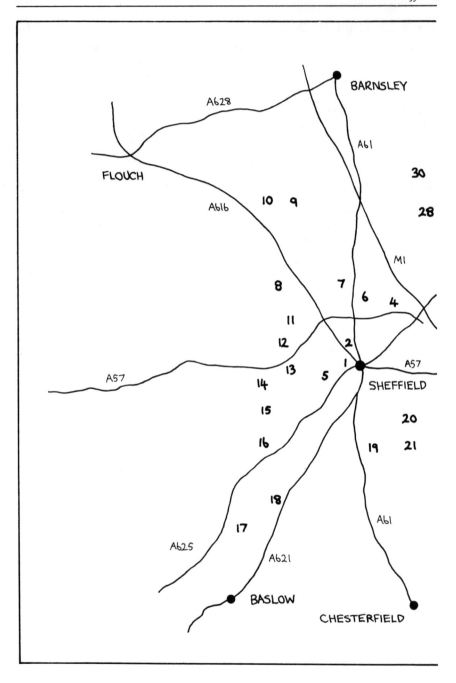

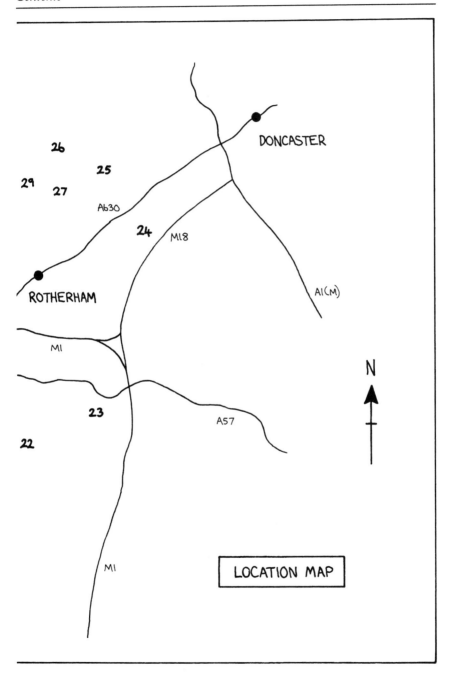

Introduction

Researching this book has taken me back to my roots. I was born in a small mining village just beyond the Sheffield boundary, so my earliest memories of the city are of shopping trips and visits to the pantomime. For me it was a place of magic and enchantment but, during my teenage years, cynicism crept in. As a regular week-end cyclist heading for the mecca of the Peak District I had to endure the tedious journey along cobbled roads from Rotherham, a journey made even more hazardous by the presence of tram lines down the centre of the road.

I became aware of the back-to-back housing in Brightside and Atter-cliffe and of the steelworks which formed a vast industrial canyon from Templeborough almost to the city centre. It was always a relief to reach the Rivelin Valley or Totley.

Occasional visits during the intervening years have allowed me to appreciate the changes that have been made to transform the environment of Sheffield, changes often occasioned by industrial decline and subsequently helped by financial assistance from the City Council, Central Government and the European Community. However, only by walking the streets, alleyways and paths for this book have I really discovered what Sheffield is really like in the 1990s. If you follow in my footsteps I hope that you, too, will quickly lose the impression that it is "an ugly picture in a beautiful frame".

As a person who loves the moors and mountains, I was reluctant initially to undertake this task. However, once I had embarked on it my eyes were opened to the many attractions of city walking. Wherever you step there is history all around you: there are architectural gems and intriguing street names. Even within the city boundary there are attractive parks and rural areas.

Getting About

Sheffield offers one great advantage for the walker: there is no problem with public transport. Wherever you start or finish it will be served by bus, train or Supertram.

Public Transport

Bus and Train Information Hotline: Sheffield (01742) 768688.
Supertram: Sheffield (01742) 767575.

Tourist Information

Tourist Information Centre, Peace Gardens. Open Mondays to Fridays, 9.30 a.m. to 5.15 p.m. and Saturdays 9.30 a.m. to 4.15 p.m. Phone: Sheffield (01742) 734671/2

Tourist Information Centre, Station Concourse. Open as above. Phone: Sheffield (0742) 795901

Tourist Information Centre, Meadowhall. Open Mondays to Thursdays 10.00 a.m. to 8.00 p.m.; Fridays 10.00 a.m. to 9.00 p.m.; Saturdays 9.00 a.m. to 7.00 p.m.

History

Like Rome, Sheffield claims to be built on seven hills: certainly it is surrounded by high ground on three sides. The highest point, High Nebb on the city boundary along Stanage Edge, reaches 1,502 feet above sea level balanced by a low point of 100 feet at Blackburn Meadows in the east. The Town Hall in the city centre stands at 265 feet.

The geology of the area has helped to fashion local history. The millstone grit of the western hills provided stones for grinding wheels turned by water from the numerous small streams and rivers such as the Porter, Loxley and Rivelin, flowing down from the fringes of the Peak District. The clay subsoil proved invaluable for lining the steel furnaces, which were powered by coal mined in the South Yorkshire coalfield.

For centuries, Sheffield was nothing more than a frontier village. In Celtic times it was on the edge of the territory of the Brigantes who constructed the hill fort at Wincobank, the only one in Europe now within a city boundary. They also bequeathed several place names including 'Wales', meaning 'foreigner'.

The Roman were responsible for taking their road from Buxton to Templeborough over Stanage by the Long Causeway and across the River Don by what is now Lady's Bridge. After their withdrawal the village, as it then was, straddled the divide between the Saxon kingdoms of Mercia and Northumbria which is commemorated by the name Meers Brook, meaning "frontier river".

Subsequently the Normans erected a castle, no longer visible, and a parish church, now the Cathedral and granted the citizens certain privileges with the Furnival Charter of 1297. By the later Middle Ages farmers were adding to their meagre incomes by grinding cutlery and other sharp-edged tools with the first mention of a Sheffield knife being contained in Chaucer's "Canterbury Tales".

Mary Queen of Scots was kept a prisoner in the Castle by Queen Elizabeth I for 14 years. In 1624 the Company of Master Cutlers was established by Act of Parliament to protect the local trade. In the eighteenth century, local industry was given a boost by Benjamin Huntsman, with his invention of Crucible Steel, and by Thomas Bolsover, who discovered the process for manufacture of Sheffield Plate. The nineteenth century saw the development of the heavy steel industry and the rise of the gigantic factories in the east of the city which generated much of the wealth of Sheffield until after the second world war. The rise of modern technology has seen the partial demise of these although in 1994 Sheffield was producing larger quantities of steel per year than during the Second World War. As a consequence of economic changes, however, the city is having to move in new directions as it enters the 21st century.

It has already proved its adaptability by attracting modern industry, replacing its acres of slum housing by award winning alternatives and landscaping deserts of industrial waste lands. The flagship of this initiative is undoubtedly the Meadowhall Centre, built on the site of a former steel works.

The Sheffield Tram

The tram figures largely in Sheffield's recent history, being one of the last places in the country to end this method of urban transport. The people were always proud of their system which in its heyday in 1927 boasted 421 vehicles some of which climbed to a height of 729 feet at Netherfield Road. Their livery of dark blue and cream, which never changed, gave them a distinctive and clean appearance in a city noted for the smoke and dirt generated by heavy industry until the coming of the clean air legislation.

The first horse-drawn trams appeared on the streets of Sheffield in 1873 with a line from Lady's Bridge to Attercliffe, a route not dissimilar from the first for the Supertram. This was followed four years later by linking the city centre with Hillsborough and Moorhead with Heeley.

In those early days, the tracks were owned by the Corporation but the trams were operated by a private company. In 1896 the city took complete control when plans were drawn-up for electrification. A generator was built on Kelham Island and the first electric car ran from Tinsley to Nether Edge on the 5th September, 1899. Six years later the tramway systems of Sheffield and neighbouring Rotherham were linked at Tinsley so that a through service could be provided.

With the rise of the petrol- and diesel-driven bus the tramway system began to decline, Sheffield's last tram running in October 1966.

1994 saw the return of the tram to the streets of Sheffield. When complete the 29 kilometre network of the Supertram will have cost £240 million. Each of the £1 million vehicles, built in Germany, will carry 88 passengers and the system, when completed, is expected to transport 20 million passengers a year.

The first trams link the city centre with Meadowhall and later extensions will operate to Mosbrough in the south and Middlewood in the north.

The Walks

This collection of pub walks in Sheffield has been compiled with a view to illustrating not only the historical heritage of this famous city but also the beauty of its numerous public parks and semi-rural areas still to be found within the city limits or just beyond its boundaries. At no point will you be more than 12 miles from the Town Hall, often very much closer. Some are designed to explore the inner core of the city with its network of narrow streets which were once lined by cutlers' workshops. Others highlight some of the famous buildings of which Sheffield is justly proud. Others will astonish the stranger by the peace and tranquillity they offer without having to travel further afield to the Peak District National Park. Indeed, while remaining completely within the Sheffield boundary one or two of the routes reach into the National Park, a sure testimony to the quality of the landscape and wildlife. Because of the nature of this particular book, few of the walks are longer than five miles: many are considerably shorter. The topography has dictated several steep climbs but there are some which are little more than gentle strolls. All can be accomplished within half a day and most are suitable for families with small children. A few are linear but, with a public transport system of the quality of Sheffield's, these present no problems about returning to the starting point or the city centre.

Summary of Walks

Walk	Location	Distance	Pub
1.	City Centre	2½ miles	Tap & Spile
2.	Kelham Island	3 miles	Fat Cat
3.	Rotherham	4 miles	Bridge Inn
4.	Meadowhall	2½ miles	Sheffield Arms
5.	Tapton	5½ miles	King's Head
6.	Concord Park	3½ miles	Travellers' Inn
7.	Ecclesfield	3 miles	Black Bull
8.	Grenoside	3 miles	Norfolk Arms
9.	Wortley	3¼ miles	Wortley Arms
10.	Greenmoor	4½ miles	Rock
11.	Loxley	3½ miles	Rose & Crown
12.	Malin Bridge	4¼ miles	Robin Hood
13.	Rivelin	4 miles	Bell Hagg
14.	Lodge Moor	5 miles	Sportsman
15.	Porter Brook	6¼ miles	Norfolk Arms.
16.	Abbeydale	3½ miles	Dore Junction
17.	Owler Bar	7¼ miles	Peacock
18.	Totley	3¼ miles	Crown
19.	Graves Park	3½ miles	New Inn
20.	Shire Brook	3 miles	Golden Plover
21.	Ridgeway	4½ miles	Old Harrow
22.	Ford	4 miles	Bridge Inn
23.	Rother Valley	4¼ miles	Angel
24.	Conisborough	7 miles	Hill Top
25.	High Melton	6 miles	Crown
26.	Clayton	5 miles	Thurnscoe
27.	Swinton	3 miles	Woodman *Bell Inn.*
28.	Wentworth	6 miles	Rockingham Arms
29.	Elsecar	3½ miles	Milton Arms
30.	Jump	4 miles	Elephant & Castle

The Pubs

The pubs are as varied as the walks. They range from the city centre variety to the cosy countryside hostelry. Where possible they have been selected for the quality of their ales and the warmth of their greeting. Most offer meals and many welcome children into their special rooms or beer gardens where play areas are provided. Remember that the provision of food is often vital for the landlord in keeping his pub viable so don't attempt to eat your own sandwiches in the bar. Most pubs now enjoy the luxury of carpeted floors so it is advisable to remove your muddy boots before entering.

Remember that this is not a National Park and the pubs therefore will often not be accustomed to catering for walkers but, as long as you observe the common courtesies you will be made more than welcome. The information regarding the beers and opening times is correct at the time of writing but these days changes are rapid so that when you call you may discover a new landlord supplied by a different brewery and operating different opening hours. All the landlords have been consulted and all are aware that they are being mentioned in this book.

Equipment

With one exception (Walk 17) none of these routes traverses lonely and exposed moorland and so offer none of the more extreme risks to be encountered in areas such as the Peak District, Lake District or the Scottish Highlands. A few, (Walks 1, 2 and 6) are along pavements or surfaced paths so they can be walked in ordinary shoes. Most, however, follow field paths, tracks and bridleways which may be muddy or rough and so require stout walking shoes or boots.

Sheffield enjoys similar weather to the neighbouring Peak District which means that it can rain. Therefore, it is advisable to carry some form of protective clothing even in the city centre. On the other hand the sun often blesses Sheffield and you may even acquire a tan.

Whatever the weather I hope that you will enjoy these walks and agree with me that Sheffield has much to offer the walker, even the most seasoned of backpackers.

Walk 1. City Centre

A tour of the heart of modern Sheffield centred on its major buildings and landmarks.

Route: Railway station – Pond Street -- Fitzalan Square – Castlegate – Church Street – Pinstone Street – Norfolk Row – Tudor Square – Howard Street – Railway Station.

Start: The Railway Station. Map reference 358870

Finish: The Railway Station. Map reference 358870

Distance: 2½ miles

Maps: 1. "Sheffield", number 743 in the Ordnance Survey's "Pathfinder" series. 2. City Centre Street Plan available from the Tourist Office

Public Transport: The railway station has services from most major cities including London, Manchester, Birmingham. Newcastle, York, Edinburgh, Norwich, Hull, Liverpool, Leeds and Doncaster. There is an extensive network of local trains. The Pond Street Interchange is served by frequent and regular buses from the suburbs and surrounding towns.

By Car: Sheffield is at the hub of a network of major trunk roads. It may be reached from junctions 30, 31, 32, 33, 34 and 35 of the M1. There are several car parks in the city centre.

Refreshments: There is a wide choice of catering establishments along the route.

Museums: The Graves Art Gallery is located within the Central Library and houses an extensive collection of British Art from the sixteenth century onwards. Opening Times: All year, Monday to Saturday 10.00 a.m. to 5.00 p.m. Closed Sunday. **The Ruskin Gallery** in Norfolk Street, opened in 1983, holds the collection of watercolours, drawings, manuscripts and books started in 1875 by the author John Ruskin. Opening Times: All year Monday to Saturday 10.00 a.m. to 5.00 p.m. Sunday: Closed.

The Tap and Spile

The Tap and Spile stands at the junction of Waingate with Castlegate and Bridge Street, almost on the site of the city's original castle and approximately half way through the walk. It is almost directly opposite Whitbread's Exchange Brewery but that is the only connection because this typically Victorian inner city pub concentrates on Real Ales, what licensee Peter Snelgrove describes as his "special expertise".

When I called it had clocked-up a grand total of 445 different brews and the barman offered me a choice between nine including Theakston's XB, Hobby Bitter from the Cotleigh Brewery, Eagle IPA from Charles Wells, Black Sheep's Special Strong and Marston's Copper Ale.

The atmosphere is redolent of the early years of this century with a large L-shaped bar lined with red leather banquettes. It is furnished with highly polished small round tables each supported by a single cast-iron leg which is balanced by three clawed feet.

The wooden bar is decorated with glazed tiles while the narrow gallery above is lined with books. The brick fireplace is matched by

areas of bare brick wall. There is a stuffed grey squirrel in a glass cage while the walls accommodate a display of mixed antique prints featuring soldiers, boxers, animals and even music hall artists. A second bar, with a raised platform at one end and one wall decorated with three cask-ends, is furnished in similar style but is reserved for non-smokers.

The unusual name of this hostelry refers to the wooden tap inserted into the cask while the "spile" is the instrument for making the spike-hole.

Opening Times: Mondays to Saturdays: 11.30 a.m. to 3.00 p.m.; 5.30 p.m. to 11 p.m.; Sundays: Closed at lunch time; 7.00 p.m. to 10.30 p.m.; Bar meals are served daily.

The Tap and Spile

The Route

On leaving the station entrance use the Pelican crossing to the far pavement of Sheaf Street before making a right turn along the pedestrian walkway so that the Nelson Mandela Building of Sheffield's Hallam University is on your immediate left. Continue as far as Pond Street bus station, exercising extreme caution while crossing the minor road used by buses.

Maintain your direction through the terminus and then the Sheffield Interchange, a small arcade of shops, to emerge by a complicated road junction facing the Post Office buildings and the Penny Black Pub. Fork left for a very easy short climb up the inappropriately named Flat Street which leads to Fitzalan Square.

Using a sign to the markets as direction finder, keep to the right-hand side of the Square, first crossing to the end of Commercial Street before entering the Haymarket, instantly recognised by a multi-coloured arch proclaiming "Castlegate". Under this continue forwards into Waingate, noticing the old Crown Court building on your left.

At the far end, Waingate forms a junction with Bridge Street, Castlegate and the Wicker. Castle Market is on your immediate right and, as the name implies, occupies the site of the ancient Sheffield Castle.

Prior to 1066 there was a Saxon hall but after the Norman Conquest, this was replaced by a motte-and-bailey castle of earth ramparts protected by a timber palisade, a section of which flanked Waingate.

Whitbread's Brewery opposite stands on land where the town mill operated from Norman times until the nineteenth century. The facing bridge, spanning the River Don, is the modern successor to the medieval Lady's Bridge, a vital communication link which provided the key for Sheffield's future economic development as a commercial centre for the surrounding area.

Turn left into Bridge Street but, after a little over 100 yards and with the new court buildings on your right, turn left into Snig Hill. At the first traffic lights and with the Co-op on your immediate left, stay forward though veering slightly to the right into Angel Street.

By the next junction, with the House of Fraser prominent, swing right into High Street, maintaining direction as it becomes Church Street. Soon the Anglican Cathedral is on your right.

It is possible that a Mercian cross, a large fragment of which is now in the British Museum, was used as the focal point of worship from as early as the ninth century. The first church was built on the same site by William de Lovelot, Lord of the Manor, in the early twelfth century

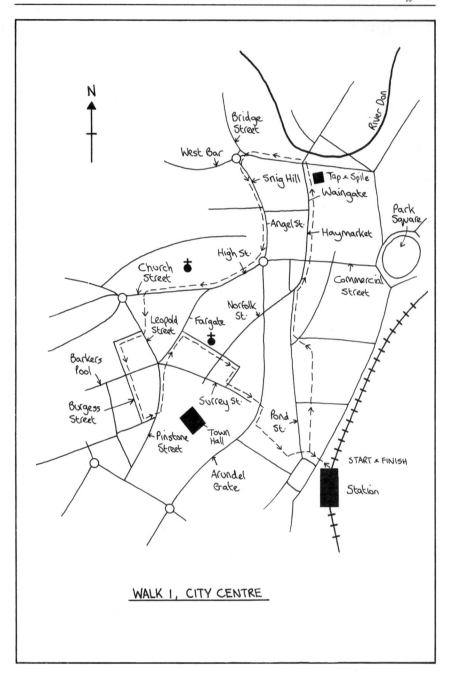

WALK 1, CITY CENTRE

and some of the actual stones from this original building are conspicuous in the east wall of the Sanctuary.

In 1430 the original church was replaced by the present one constructed in the Perpendicular style. Over the centuries various alterations and extensions have been made but none more drastic than those of 1966 when the modern entrance and Narthex Tower were added to upgrade the former parish church into a cathedral resulting from the creation of the Sheffield Diocese in 1914.

The building is noted for its stained glass windows dating from various periods of history, a 15th century oak screen and the tombs of the fourth and fifth Earls of Shrewsbury who were Lords of the Manor of Sheffield. Amongst several famous people to visit the church was

Mary, Queen of Scots while she was staying at the Castle as a prisoner of Queen Elizabeth I with the sixth Earl of Shrewsbury as her appointed custodian.

On the opposite side of Church Street to the Cathedral stands the Victorian Cutlers' Hall, a large, well proportioned stone building with Greek columns. It is the third hall to carry that name since the Cutlers' Company was established by Act of Parliament in 1624. During the previous century many cutlers had been developing their own marks, all protected in the Manorial Court, but, with trade expanding it was considered necessary to obtain stronger control over the industry.

Sheffield Cathedral

From the Cathedral, continue along Church Street for a short distance before, by the Leicester Building Society, making a left turn into Orchard Street, a reminder perhaps that until the end of the eighteenth century Sheffield was little more than a village. Allow a few minutes for turning into Orchard Square to browse round the shops and to enjoy some light refreshments. With its sharp red brickwork and decorated chiming clock, it is like stepping from Sheffield into the heart of a Dutch town.

Regaining Orchard Street continue to the end before crossing Leopold Street diagonally left to enter Orchard Lane with the Education Offices on your right and the glass and tile Fountain Precinct on your left. By the corner of the Precinct make a left turn into Balm Green soon emerging into Barker's Pool by the City Hall, an imposing neo-classical building used as a venue for concerts of classical music and perform-ances by rock and pop groups. In front is the bronze War Memorial with the badges of several local regiments.

Cross Barker's Pool to walk between Mothercare and Cole Brothers into Burgess Street and, at the far end, turn left along Cross Burgess Street for 20 yards to reach Pinstone Street opposite the Peace Gardens.

Turn left to pass in front of the imposing Town Hall, completed in 1896 and opened by Queen Victoria the following year. Maintain the same line of direction through Barker's Pool, named after an enterpris-ing citizen who, several centuries ago, created the pool to provide residents with a water supply.

Cross to Fargate and then take the first turn on the right to enter Norfolk Row where you will find the Roman Catholic Cathedral of St. Marie. When conditions eased for Roman Catholics in the eighteenth century a large chapel was built on this site, then partially occupied by a house owned by the agent of the Duke of Norfolk, a prominent Catholic himself. By the middle of the nineteenth century this church proved too small and was demolished to allow for the construction of the present church. This was opened in 1850 and elevated to the status of a Cathedral when the new Roman Catholic Diocese of Hallam was created in 1980 thus making Sheffield one of the few cities in this country to have both an Anglican and Roman Catholic cathedral. Its design is based on a study of several fourteenth century churches and the interior is striking for the quality of its stained glass windows and a Reredos by Pugin.

Leave Norfolk Row by crossing Norfolk Street into Tudor Square, now pedestrianised and home to the Sheffield theatres including, on your left, the Crucible, a modern building with a repertory company and, for television addicts, the international spiritual home of snooker. Ahead is the Lyceum, dating from 1897 and recently renovated and refurbished to stage major productions of drama, opera and music by touring companies.

On coming face-to-face with the Lyceum turn right to walk by Central Library, a white building which also houses the Graves Art Gallery with its collection of British and European paintings from the sixteenth century onwards.

By the corner of the library turn left into Surrey Street. Soon, on your right, you will pass Leader House, a fine example of Georgian architecture built by the Duke of Norfolk for Vincent Eyre.

Swing right into Arundel Gate but, after 20 yards and by the Novotel, descend the flight of steps leading into the subway. Leaving the short underground tunnel stay forward down the path which runs parallel to Howard Street with the Science Park obvious on your right and, almost opposite, the Nelson Mandela Building of Hallam University. At the foot of the hill, use the Pelican crossing in negotiating the busy Sheaf Street to regain the station entrance.

Walk 2. Kelham Island

A linear route commencing in the modern city centre before entering an area typical of Sheffield's nineteenth century industry with its small scale factories and cutlers' shops.

Route: Fitzalan Square – West Bar – Alma Street – Kelham Island – Cotton Street – Green Lane – Neepsend Lane – Waterloo Walk – Shales Moor.

Start: Fitzalan Square. Map reference 357875

Finish: The junction of Penistone Road with Shales Moor. Map Reference 349881

Distance: 3 miles

Maps: 1. "Sheffield", number 743 in the Ordnance Survey's "Pathfinder" series. 2. A to Z Sheffield Street Atlas.

Public Transport: The start is served by Supertram and by frequent buses from the city centre and some suburbs.

By Car: There are several city centre car parks and one at the Kelham Island Museum.

Refreshments: There are several cafes and pubs around Fitzalan Square and along the route. The Cat Fat is adjacent to the Kelham Island Museum where there is also a cafe.

Museums: Kelham Island Museum houses exhibits associated with the industrial history of the area. **Opening Times:** Monday to Thursday 10.00 a.m. to 4.00 p.m.; Sunday 11.00 a.m. to 4.00 p.m.; Closed Fridays and Saturdays throughout the year and from; December 6th to March 5th inclusive. **The South Yorkshire Fire Museum** is located at West Bar and illustrates the story of the fire service. **Opening Times:** Sundays all year from 11.00 a.m. to 5.00 p.m. Phone: Sheffield (01742) 752147.

The Fat Cat

Situated approximately half way through this walk, the Fat Cat is adjacent to Kelham Island Industrial Museum. Once a part of the Alma Hotel, it now encapsulates the atmosphere of a typical small pub that was to be found in the midst of the dirty and dusty factories in the second half of the nineteenth century and the early part of the twentieth.

Sit in the bar at lunch-time or early evening and you expect to see cutlers or steel workers filing in through the door, eager to slake their thirst after a morning or afternoon constantly inhaling the dust from their grindstones or exposed to the fierce heat of the furnaces.

There are some differences, of course. The bar, very tiny and L-shaped, is carpeted. Plush settle seats line the walls and the small, round tables with their wooden tops add to the atmosphere. The walls carry displays of black and white photographs showing men at work in local factories and the tiny cutlers' workshops that were once a feature of the Kelham Island area.

On tap when I called was a selection of real ales including K. W. Special from the Concertina Brewery, Royal Oak brewed by Eldridge Pope in Dorchester and Marston's Owd Roger and Mother's Ruin. Add

to these Theakston's Old Peculier, Timothy Taylor's Landlord and a whole range of bottled brews including Chimay Blue and Kwak. Pride of place, however must go to Kelham Island Brewery's Best Bitter which is brewed in the Fat Cat's own back yard along with Hallamshire Bitter and Celebration Ale. These unusual beers are matched by a selection of country wines including cowslip, dandelion and rhubarb and piquant bar snacks such as leek pie, pepper and mushroom casserole and jam and treacle sponge.

Opening Times: Monday to Saturday 12.00 noon to 3.00 p.m. and 5.30 p.m. to 10.30 p.m.; Sunday 12.00 noon to 3.00 p.m. and 7.00 p.m. to 10.30 p.m.

The Fat Cat

The Route

Starting from Fitzalan Square, this route is a journey back in time from
the busy, bustling, modern, rejuvenated city centre into one of the
oldest industrial districts of Sheffield, once a labyrinth of narrow
cobbled streets lined with small factories and tiny workshops. Much of
this atmosphere has been retained with several of the nineteenth
century workshops still standing.

Leave Fitzalan square by way of High Street but, at the Market Place
after 100 yards, swing right into Angel Street for a distance of some 200
yards. At the first set of traffic lights veer left down Snig Hill, which
derives its name from the gadgets once used to slow down or brake the
descent of carts. At the foot of the hill turn left into West Bar with the
new Law Courts on your right.

By West Bar Green, facing the red-brick South Yorkshire Fire Museum, look out for the tourist sign to Kelham Island and turn right into
Corporation Street, soon passing the South Yorkshire Ambulance Service workshops on your left. Continue to the far end, crossing the bridge
spanning the River Don.

By the set of traffic lights make a right turn into Nursery Street,
walking for approximately 250 yards until opposite the New Testament
Church of God Incorporated. At that point look across the river and you
will see the goit, which was built to create Kelham Island, re-joining the
River Don. Even here, where there is a fair amount of litter being carried
along the by current, it is still possible to come across parties of mallard
swimming about.

Retrace your steps to the traffic lights before turning left into Corporation Street and re-crossing the bridge. At the next set of traffic lights
make a right turn into Alma Street and then continue for several
hundred yards, passing a number of small factories and workshops to
reach Kelham Island Museum on your right. Turn right into the car
park, cross the small bridge over the goit and follow the signs to the
official entrance.

The building in which the museum is housed was erected in 1897 as
a power station to provide electricity for the first of Sheffield's electric
trams. This replaced a former iron works where the boneshaker bicycle
which is displayed in the museum was made. The museum uses
artefacts and displays to illustrate the history of Sheffield's industry
from the first cutlers through to the giant steelworks and coal mines of
this century.

Life-size models of living and working conditions have been created
but for many, the highlight will be watching the last of the traditional

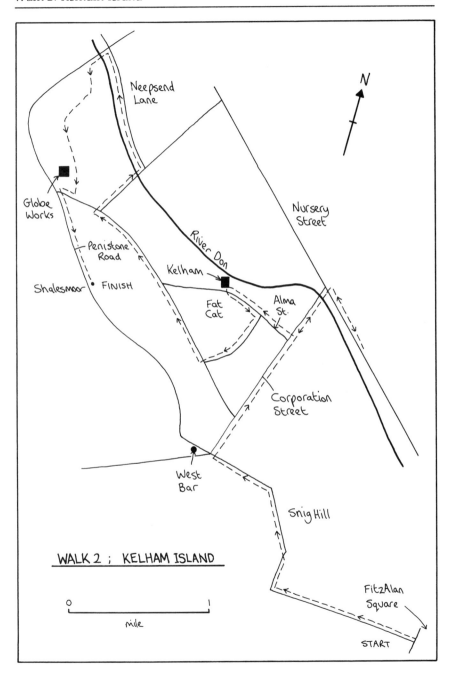

Neepsend Lane

N

Globe Works

Nursery Street

River Don

Penistone Road

Kelham

Shalesmoor • FINISH

Fat Cat

Alma St.

Corporation Street

West Bar

Snig Hill

WALK 2 ; KELHAM ISLAND

0   1

mile

FitzAlan Square

START

cutlers at work fashioning their knives, saws, sharp-edged tools and guillotine blades. These may be purchased directly although these "Little Mesters" still actually produce for outside markets where quality is the hall mark. Notice the enormous Bessemer Converter in the yard: it was this type of furnace which transformed Sheffield's steel industry and generated so much of its wealth.

When Dam Dyke Reservoir burst its retaining wall in 1864 the area around Kelham Island suffered enormous damage as a huge wall of water swept down the valley of the Don. The force of water was such that several gigantic grindstones were swept away, never to be recovered, a grinding hull was destroyed and three cottages suffered irreparable damage.

Leaving the museum turn right for the few yards to the Fat Cat. Suitably refreshed, make a left turn from the entrance and retrace your steps along Alma Street before turning right down Cotton Street, another reminder of the variety of industry associated with Sheffield in times past.

Narrow and cobbled, the street runs between brick walls and windowless factory backs. As you walk along keep an eye open for numerous minor relics of the industrial heritage such as cast iron and enamelled signs, gas lamps, stone pavements, discarded grindstones and ornamentation on factory buildings.

At the end of Cotton Street go right along Bower Street but, after 75 yards, make another right turn into Russell Street which is recognised by its large Ford garage. By the Cornwall Works bear left into Green Lane, noticing an old stone-built Board School of 1883 which is now converted into a small factory producing nuts, bolts and screws.

Further along, on your right, comes the Green Lane Works with its imposing classical entrance surmounted by an ornamental clock tower complete with cupola. Hereabouts the pavement, recently renovated, has been relaid with traditional gritstone flagstones.

Beyond the Green Lane Works turn right into Ball Street, passing the now derelict "Steel, Saw and File Works" before crossing Ball Street Bridge. Looking to your right you will see an enormous weir and, further downstream Kelham Island. Beyond the bridge take the first turning on the left, Lancaster Street, and, at the junction with Neepsend Lane, maintain direction taking a distant gasometer and ski-slope as your guidestones.

Soon the River Don is flowing immediately on your left but, opposite the Cannon Brewery of William Stones and at the junction of Neepsend Lane with Burton Road, turn sharp left over a bridge into Rutland Road.

By the far end of the bridge, and before reaching the conspicuous building of Samuel Osborn Steel Makers on the opposite side of the road, make a sharp left turn onto a narrow riverside path, Waterloo Walk, which offers a good view of the old industrial buildings lining the River Don.

With its old-fashioned gas lamps, cobbles and cast-iron bollards, the path recalls a former age. Incidentally the first bollards were made by using upturned cannons with cannon balls stuffed into the muzzles. Those in Waterloo Walk are based on this concept.

On coming face-to-face with Gate Number 9 of the West Packaging Company, turn left along Cornish Street but, at the junction with Green Lane turn right. Where this meets Penistone Road stands the Globe Works.

These were built in the second decade of the nineteenth century for the refining of steel and the manufacture of a whole range of allied objects ranging from stoves, grates and fenders to scythes, saws and files. Later in the century the business outgrew these premises so a transfer was made to the former workhouse which still stands opposite the entrance to the Kelham Island Museum.

Afterwards the Globe Works were subdivided for use by small craftsmen. The last hand file-cutter in Sheffield operated there until the 1980s. Today, the refurbished building houses a visitor centre, a small museum and a range of small businesses from graphic design to financial consultancies.

At the junction by the Globe Works turn left along Penistone Road until it meets Shales Moor where a choice of buses is available for the journey back into the city centre.

Walk 3. Canal and River

Commencing in the very heart of Rotherham this walk follows the course of the River Don and the South Yorkshire Navigation into the centre of Meadowhall, the enormous new shopping complex built on the site of a former steelworks and one of the showpieces of the rejuvenated Sheffield.

Route: The Bridge Inn – 5th Avenue – New York – Templeborough – Jordan – Tinsley Locks – Meadowhall

Start: The Bridge Inn, Rotherham. Map reference 427931.

Finish: Meadowhall Interchange. Map reference 390913.

Distance: 4 miles.

Maps: 1. "Rotherham", number 727 in the Ordnance Survey's "Pathfinder" series. 2. "Sheffield (North) & Stocksbridge", number 726 in the Ordnance Survey's "Pathfinder" series.

Public Transport: The start is served by several bus routes from the suburbs of Rotherham and surrounding towns including Sheffield, Barnsley, Doncaster and Mansfield. The Bridge Inn is only a few yards from Rotherham Central railway station for trains from Doncaster, Leeds, Sheffield and other towns. Meadowhall Interchange is the terminus for Supertram, linking it with the city centre and selected Sheffield suburbs. The Interchange has frequent and regular daily (including Sundays) trains from Rotherham, Cleethorpes, Sheffield, Doncaster, Stockport, Leeds, Manchester, Barnsley and York. In addition there are frequent bus services from various districts of Sheffield and towns further afield.

By Car: Several major roads from Barnsley, Doncaster and Sheffield converge on Rotherham. Meadowhall is signed from the M1 (Junction 34 South) and (Junction 34 North), in addition to the A631, the A6102, the A6109 and the A6178. There are several large car parks in Rotherham town centre and at Meadowhall.

Refreshments: There is a wide selection of restaurants, cafes and pubs in both Rotherham and Meadowhall.

The Bridge Inn

The Bridge Inn near the centre of Rotherham has long been associated with the bridge spanning the River Don from which it takes its name.

The original inn was built in the late eighteenth century, probably 1778, by William Ridgeway, a butcher by trade. The present building is the result of a complete reconstruction about 1930 when the new Chantry Bridge was erected alongside the medieval bridge to cope with increasing traffic. It is mainly of stone construction, with one end rounded, but with a small section of magpie architecture and brick chimneys.

Indeed, inside there is a map dated 1853 showing the inn already in existence. In the Chantry Lounge, named after the old chapel on the bridge, there is a picture showing the pub at some unspecified date with an advertisement for Mappin's Beers painted on the end of the building.

Inside, the first bar is small, partially rounded to fit in with the outside walls. It has a cosy, friendly atmosphere not always to be found in town centre pubs. The landlord, Edward Walsham serves Stones Best Bitter and Bass on hand pump and also serves a wide selection of bar meals.

For those wishing to escape to a quiet corner there is the Chantry Lounge with its old pictures, thick wooden beams, etching, also of the Bridge Inn, and the seating is on banquettes.

Opening Times: Mons-Sats: 10.30 a.m. to 3.00 p.m. and 6.00 p.m. to 11.00 p.m.; Suns: 12.00 a.m. to 3.00 p.m. and 7.00 p.m. to 10.30 p.m.; Bar meals Mons-Sats. 12.00 a.m. to 2.00 p.m. Sandwiches in the evenings and Saturday lunch time.

The Bridge Inn

Rotherham

The route begins from Rotherham Bridge which has provided a vital river crossing for several centuries, thereby guaranteeing Rotherham's importance as a communication centre. The bridge is unusual in that it boasts a chapel, one of only three such bridges in the country. The other two are to be seen at Wakefield, also in Yorkshire, and at St. Ives in Cambridgeshire.

Dedicated to Our Lady, the chapel dates from medieval times, first being mentioned in the will of John Bokyng in 1483. Completely without endowments the chapel and its priest relied on offerings and donations from travellers for its upkeep. After the Dissolution of the Monasteries in 1540 by Henry VIII, it ceased to be used for worship and, subsequently served as a gaol, an almshouse and a tobacconist's shop. It was rescued from similar uses in 1924 when it was reconsecrated and it now has a weekly communion service.

The nearby town centre is dominated by the pinnacled tower of its parish church, All Saints, which has occupied the site since 1409. It serves as a reminder that Rotherham was an important seat of learning during the late medieval period thanks to the College of Jesus, founded by a native son, Archbishop Thomas Holgate, in 1482. As with so many similar foundations it failed to survive the Reformation.

The first ironworks in the town were established by Samuel Walker in 1746 after which Rotherham boomed economically with coal mining and the manufacture of brass, steel and similar products. Its goods reached their markets along the South Yorkshire Navigation which linked it with Hull until it was superseded by the railways during the middle years of the nineteenth century.

The Route

Emerging from the Bridge Inn, cross the busy road junction to enter the facing College Road. A short distance beyond Rotherham Central Station on your left and by the Phoenix Hotel, turn left into Masbrough Road which is signed as a cul-de-sac. This leads through a small modern industrial estate and, while there is no exit for motorised traffic, there is for pedestrians. By this exit turn left in front of The Travellers pub to cross the end of Main Street into Brinsworth Street. On your immediate left is a night club, "5th Avenue", a rather appropriate name because this area is known as New York.

Where the busy A630 on your right starts to climb, stay left along Brinsworth Street which soon turns right to pass beneath the A630. Immediately, and facing an aluminium re-cycling works, fork left again

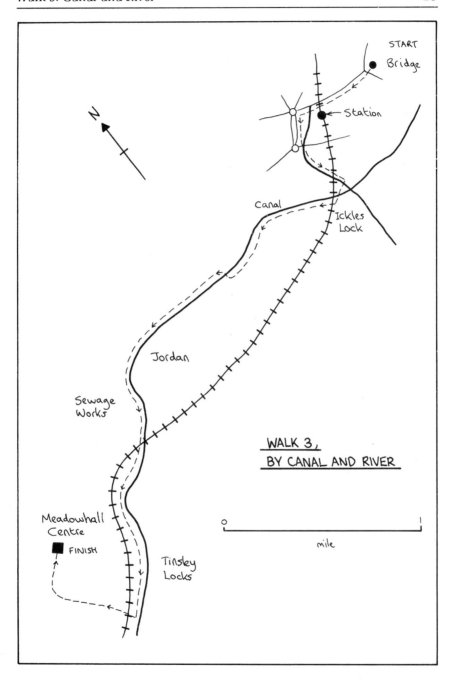

so that the railway is close to your left. After a further 250 yards make a sharp left turn over a level crossing and continue over the canal until reaching a modern bungalow on your right. By the far corner of this turn right to reach Ickles Lock, following the recently renovated towpath to the left of the South Yorkshire Canal.

On your left, but no longer visible, is the site of the ancient Roman Fort of Templeborough which was linked by roads with Brough in the Hope Valley, Buxton and Glossop. More recently it was occupied by the Templeborough Steel Works but, thanks to Government and European money, is in process of being landscaped and thereby improving the appearance of the area.

Pass beneath a green metal railway bridge supported by arches and, within 40 yards, walk under a second but this one grey in colour and standing on thick, round metal pillars. Soon the first lock is encountered. Climb slightly, turn right over a narrow bridge and then turn left along a broad track so that the canal is on your left.

Soon the towpath is lined with scattered silver birch but the most surprising sight is that of several sheep grazing in a small field on your right before you pass beneath a large metal pipe to gain Jordan Top Lock.

To the left the River Don flows over an extremely large weir but, from this point onwards river and canal join for the next mile upstream to Tinsley Locks. At Jordan Lock, turn right over a small black metal footbridge and then turn left so that two cooling towers are visible directly ahead. After 100 yards, where the path forms a Y-junction, fork left, staying to the right of the river as it enters into an enormous bend with a sewage works on your immediate right.

Having passed under another gun-metal grey bridge you may encounter a party of mallards on the water and will certainly hear blackbirds, starlings and blue tits if you pass this way during spring and early summer. Along this section, our route is along a typical towpath as it passes beneath two more large overhead pipes in quick succession and yet another grey bridge. The path leads directly onto a narrow concrete bridge over the river before arriving at the first of the Tinsley series of locks.

With canal and River Don separate once again, stay to the right of the canal which acquires a wide, surfaced path and street lights before passing directly under the M1 motorway. One hundred yards beyond, and by the far corner of some derelict red-brick buildings, leave the canal by forking right up a broad track to reach a main road.

Turn right over the railway but, at the first traffic island with traffic lights, turn right again into the Meadowhall Shopping Centre. Follow the signs to the Interchange unless, of course, you wish to browse around amongst the hundred of shops.

Walk 4. Meadowhall

An unexpectedly rural route which transports us back in time from the late twentieth century shopping complex of Meadowhall to the Iron Age hill fort of Wincobank, revealing a little of the intervening centuries in the process.

Route: Meadowhall Interchange – Low Wincobank – Roman Ridge – Wincobank Wood – Grimesthorpe

Start: Meadowhall Interchange. Map reference 390913

Finish: The corner of Upwell Street and Holywell Road, Grimesthorpe. Map reference 378901.

Distance: 2½ miles.

Map: "Sheffield (North) and Stocksbridge", number 726 in the Ordnance Survey's "Pathfinder" series.

Public Transport: Meadowhall Interchange is served by the Supertram from the city centre and by trains from Sheffield, Rotherham, Leeds, York, Barnsley, Doncaster, Manchester, Stockport and Cleethorpes. Buses also serve the city centre and many of the outlying suburbs and surrounding towns. The finish is served by several bus routes to the city centre.

By Car: Meadowhall Interchange is signed from Junction 34 (North) and Junction 34 (South) on the M1. It is also signed from the A631, A6102, A6109 and A6178. There are several large car parks.

Refreshments: There is a selection of cafes and restaurants at Meadowhall. None on the route.

The Sheffield Arms

With its bright exterior decor and sign, the Sheffield Arms is conspicuous amongst its rather drab surroundings in the appropriately named Grimesthorpe district of Sheffield.

Inside, a central bar serves two rooms, one somewhat larger than the other which has the snug, friendly atmosphere normally associated with more rural hostelries. The walls are decorated with a Laura Ashley type paper, the floor is carpeted and the brick fireplace is adorned by two old-fashioned coaching lamps.

The walls are lined with leather-covered banquettes, matched by leather-topped stools set around formica-topped tables. Surprisingly there is a selection of original oil paintings on the walls, some apparently of Paris street scenes.

Although the pub does not offer food, the landlord, Gerald Firth, serves a well-kept cask conditioned Stones Bitter which is obviously popular with the locals.

Opening Times: Mondays to Saturdays: 11.00 a.m. to 11.00 p.m.; Sundays: 12.00 a.m. to 3.00 p.m. and 7.00 p.m. to 10.30 p.m.

The Sheffield Arms

The Route

On arriving at Meadowhall Interchange turn your back on the extensive shopping malls to follow the exit signs along the walkways to Tyler Street. Cross to the far side and turn right, but only for a few yards before swinging left up a flight of concrete steps which provide access to Evesham Close, a fairly obvious modern development.

Continue climbing, rather steeply, to the junction with Aylesbury Crescent. Fork left for approximately 50 yards. By the end of the last house on your left veer even further to the left onto an unsigned but obvious path which pursues its steep relentless upwards course with

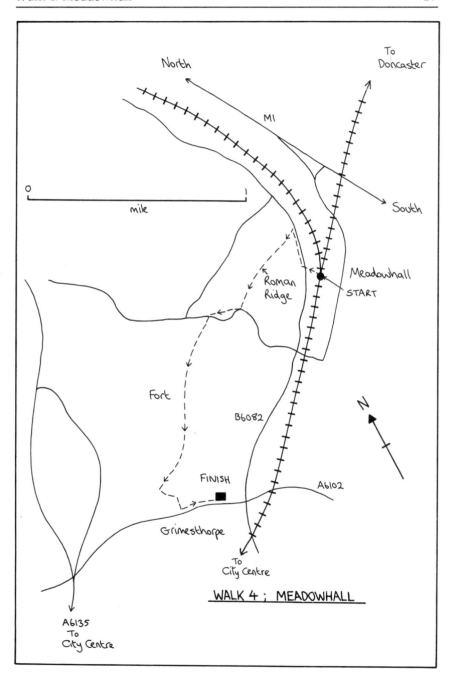

the houses of Aylesbury Crescent now on your right and several modern factory units on your left.

Within ten minutes of leaving the late twentieth century development of Meadowhall you have stepped back at least 2,000 years in time. Your path is climbing what is shown on the Ordnance Survey map as "Roman Ridge". Historians disagree about its date, some arguing that it was first pounded by human feet in the Iron Age while others regard it as the product of the Saxon period.

Perhaps all these observations are correct. It may have been an existing route taken over by the Romans as their legions marched between their fort at Templeborough, near Rotherham, and those of Navio in the Hope Valley and Melandra, near Glossop. Doubtless the later Saxons also took advantage of its existence . Whatever its origins it is still in place to be enjoyed by the walker in the age of Supertram. As it climbs to a height of 120 metres the path offers interesting views out across the former heartland of Sheffield's heavy steel industry. Some works remain, but others have now vanished, leaving enormous gaps awaiting either new developments or reclamation.

In the far distance of the lower Don Valley are the green remnants which have survived the upheavals of the last two centuries to provide some idea of the beauty of this valley as described by Sir Walter Scott who used the vicinity of Conisborough Castle as the setting for his novel "Ivanhoe".

The ridge path continues upwards passing small open patches of grassland and clumps of birch trees on your right. At the first intersection of paths maintain the line of direction until meeting Jenkin Road. Turn right along this to pass the entrances to Sandstone Road and Forthill Road, both on your left. Just beyond the second, and on the brow of the hill, make a left turn to the side of a large, black metal gate into the recently cobbled Winco Wood Lane.

This is identifiable by the large Sheffield Countryside Management notice accompanied by another announcing that this area, Wincobank Wood, forms part of the new South Yorkshire Community Forest which is sponsored by the Countryside Commission. It is rather strange to reflect that you are only about two miles from the city centre.

This rural lane continues climbing for some considerable distance providing ever-widening views out over the City of Sheffield to the moorlands encompassing it to the north and the west. On achieving the summit you look down onto a patchwork of late nineteenth and early twentieth century terraced streets, factories and open spaces. In contrast, closer to the city centre, modern high rise housing rises like skyscrapers.

In the far distance, almost as a backdrop, are the moors beyond Stocksbridge, Dore and Totley. The one breathtaking panorama provides an unrivalled perspective of the historical development of England's fourth largest city.

The flat summit where you stand is the site of Wincobank's Iron Age Fort, the only one in Europe located within a city's boundaries. It formed the centre of a political entity, the double ring of earthworks protecting primitive houses. It ranks with the Iron Age fort that once occupied the crest of Mam Tor, near Castleton, in the Peak District.

On the summit, the wide track forms a Y-junction. Take the left-hand fork to commence the long, steep descent as the path, now without cobbles, twists first to the left and then the right. Wincobank Wood, birch intermingled with oak, is away to your right.

At the first intersection of paths, adjacent to a football pitch on your left, continue forward over a footbridge constructed from railway sleepers with a distant view of Sheffield Arena directly ahead. Continue losing height until meeting a wide, surfaced track.

Turn left for 100 yards to meet Wincobank Lane by a derelict red-brick house. Turn right. At the bottom of the hill make a left turn along Upwell Street to enjoy a well earned pint in the Sheffield Arms after a mere 150 yards.

Walk 5. Tapton

A circular route meandering through the University quarter and linking several of the city's parks.

Route: Brook Hill – Weston Park – Crookes Valley Park – Tapton Hill – Endcliffe Edge – Endcliffe Park – Botanical Gardens – Brook Hill

Start: The junction of Brook Hill with Upper Hanover Street and Netherthorpe Road. Map reference 344874

Distance: 5½ miles.

Maps: 1. "Sheffield", number 743 in the Ordnance Survey's "Pathfinder" series. 2. A to Z Street Atlas of Sheffield.

Public Transport: The start may be reached by Supertram and bus number 52 from High Street.

By Car: It is more convenient to park in one of the city centre car parks and then use public transport.

Refreshments: The **King's Head** and **The Grindstone** pubs along the route both serve bar meals at lunch times and in the evenings; The Coffee Bar in the Mappin Art Gallery, Weston Park is open Tuesdays to Saturdays: 11.00 a.m. to 3.00 p.m.; Sundays: 2.00 p.m. to 4.00 p.m. Mondays: Closed. There is also a small cafe in Endcliffe Park serving beverages, cold drinks and other light refreshments.

Museums: The Mappin Art Gallery is situated in Weston Park. The permanent collection has outstanding works by eighteenth and nineteenth century British artists including the Pre-Raphaelites. Contemporary art is catered for by a series of changing exhibitions. **Opening Times:** All year: Tuesday to Saturday 10.00 a.m. to 5.00 p.m.; Sundays 2.00 p.m. to 4.15 p.m. **The City Museum** forms part of the Mappin Art Gallery, Weston Park. It has the largest collection of Sheffield Plate and cutlery in the world. There are also Bronze Age, geological and wildlife exhibits. **Opening Times:** As above. **The Traditional Heritage Museum** is located at 605 Eccleshall Road. It exhibits displays of local crafts including cutlery, clog making, file-cutting and local folklore. **Opening Times:** Restricted. telephone Sheffield (01742) 768555, Extension 6256.

The King's Head

Although the King's Head, which stands on Manchester Road, Tapton Hill, forms part of the Beefeater chain, it still manages to retain a distinct feeling of individuality. From its large windows there is a fine view southwards over Eccleshall, Millhouses and Abbeydale to the distant hills. The large bar has a raised section at one end, partitioned off with wooden posts and with beams which show signs of considerable age. This is mirrored by parts of the woodwork left exposed around some of the windows while the rendered walls and brick fireplace, complete with open fire, create a 'lived-in' atmosphere which is simultaneously warm and welcoming. To add to this old-worlde ambience the walls are adorned with copperware and a variety of sporting prints while the canopy over the bar is decorated with leaded windows. Plush banquettes line the room and are complemented by stools and polished wooden tables.

Licensee Richard Hill offers cask-conditioned Boddington's Bitter along with castle Eden Ale, Eden Bitter and a changing guest beer which, when I called, was Old Dambuster. For those with other tastes there is a splendid selection of lagers and wines. Bar meals are served daily at both lunch time and in the evenings. For those in search of something more substantial there is also a full-scale restaurant.

Opening Times: Easter to October, 11.30 a.m. to 11.00 p.m.; November to Easter 11.30 a.m. to 3.00 p.m. and 5.30 p.m. to 11.00 p.m. Sunday all day.

The King's Head

The Route

This walk offers an opportunity to savour another aspect of Sheffield's varied heritage: an inheritance of culture reflected in some of its art galleries, museums and Victorian parks. They are linked by quiet suburban roads and lanes lined with the large, elegant stone-built mansions of successful nineteenth century manufacturers and businessmen who preferred to live well away from the factories and workshops which generated their wealth.

Today these houses, often subdivided into flats, live cheek by jowl with examples of twentieth century architecture in the form of university halls of residence, yet another reflection of the on-going cultural life and energy of Sheffield.

Alighting from the bus or Supertram by the main centre of the University, where Brook Hill intersects Upper Hanover Street and Netherthorpe Road, walk up the hill away from the city centre.

Within 100 yards turn right through the cast-iron gates into Weston Park. Covering 13 acres this was acquired by the City Council for the use of its citizens in 1873. To the right is an impressive war memorial to the men of the York and Lancaster Regiment who died during the two World Wars. This is appropriate for the regiment, no longer in existence, recruited locally. A few yards further away is a statue of Ebenezer Elliot, a South Yorkshire writer who championed the working classes during the middle years of the nineteenth century. In the same vicinity is the Festival of Britain Garden and Conservatory erected in 1951.

Staying with the main drive, the Mappin Gallery, an imposing neo-classical building with porticos and columns dating from 1887, is on your left. Despite its international reputation admission has always been free. Just beyond the Mappin Gallery Europe's largest artificial ski slope at Parkwood Springs comes into the distant view but closer at hand is a white decorated column topped with an urn. Erected in 1871, it commemorates the work of Sheffield artist, Godfrey Sykes.

Continue with the rhododendrons and other shrubs on your left and tennis courts to your right. By the far corner of these fork left to exit the park onto the junction of Mushroom Lane with Crookes Valley Road. Cross Mushroom Lane directly into Crookes Valley Park. Fork left along the broad, surfaced path as it runs to the right of the bowling greens until it terminates after 150 yards.

There, turn left, descend a flight of steps and turn right at the bottom to find a large lake on your left. By the far corner of this, a few yards beyond a cream-coloured shelter, climb briefly to a metal gate. Turn left

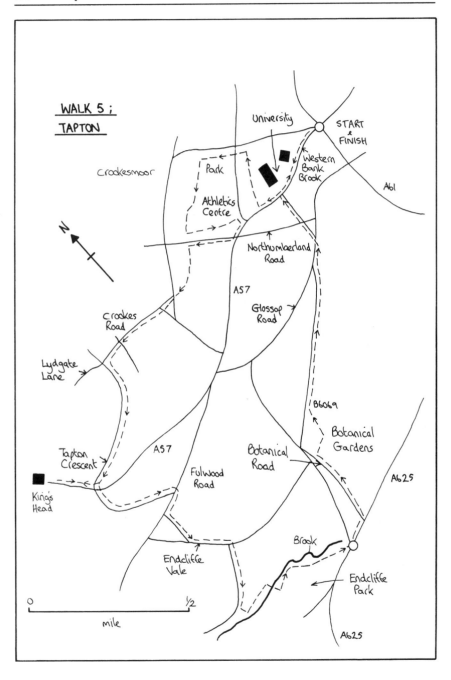

to walk behind the Damhouse Restaurant before leaving the park through a set of double gates. Turn right to a Y-junction after 60 yards and then turn left as you re-join Mushroom Lane.

Turn right for a distance of 50 yards to the complicated road junction of Mushroom Lane, Western Bank, Northumberland Road and Whitham Road.

Turn right into Northumberland Road, descending steeply for a short distance. By the first corner of the University's Northumberland Road car park make a left turn into an unsigned and very narrow walled lane.

As it climbs gently the initial cobbled surface gives way to flagging before eventually arriving at the foot of a flight of steps. At the top of these, cross directly over Crookesmoor Road into Roslin Road which ascends steeply to its junction with Crookes Road.

Turn right along this so that Tapton Hall of Residence is on your left. At the next junction keep the Grindstone pub on your right as you enter Lydgate Lane but, after a further 200 yards, make a left turn into Tapton Crescent Road. This runs along the contour and provides some fine views across the city. The property is of mixed age but several houses, including Hallam House and Hallam Lodge, reflect the wealth of their Victorian owners.

On reaching Manchester Road turn right to pass to the left of the Congregational Church as you walk for 100 yards up the slope to the King's Head. Suitably refreshed, retrace your steps before turning right for the steep, twisting descent of Shore Lane passing Ranmoor House, another University Hall of Residence, on the way.

At the foot of the slope make a right turn into Fulwood Road but leave it after approximately 100 yards by turning left into Woodvale Road with its substantial nineteenth century houses.

At the far end turn left into Endcliffe Vale Road to pass Sorby Hall on your left. Ten yards after crossing over the entrance to Endcliffe Grove Avenue make a right turn into Riverdale Road.

Where this bends sharply round to the right, turn left through a gateway into Endcliffe Park, dropping quickly down to the Porter Brook. At the first junction stay forward but, after the second, walk between the brook and the lake which, despite its proximity to the city centre, is frequented by mallard, coot, moorhen and other waterfowl.

By the far end of the lake swing to the right, cross a small ornamental stone bridge to another junction. Turn left again so that you pass to the right of the refreshment kiosk and the children's playground. Maintain the same line of direction through the park to pass an enormous statue of Queen Victoria before emerging by the large traffic island at Hunter's Bar.

Exercising extreme caution, walk round to the left of this before entering Eccleshall Road which is signed to the city centre. Opposite the Traditional Heritage Museum turn left into Botanical Road which climbs steeply to pass several side roads to narrow and descend towards Clarkehouse Road.

Immediately before the junction, however, turn right through the entrance gates into the Botanical Gardens, 18 acres of floral displays and plant collections. It is also the haunt of grey squirrels, jays, and an assortment of small songbirds.

In the gardens, turn left to walk in front of the large conservatories before making an exit into Clarkehouse Road. There turn right passing the King Edward VII School with its neo-classical facade. Further along you will pass the Royal Hallamshire Hospital.

On reaching the junction of Clarkehouse Road with Glossop Road continue in the direction of the city centre. By the West End pub turn left into Clarkson Street to meet Western Bank facing Weston Park. Turn right for the last few remaining yards to your starting point.

Walk 6. Concord

A linear walk commencing with extensive panoramic views followed by woodland and field paths to the ancient village of Ecclesfield

Route: Concord Park – Woolley Wood – Deep Lane – Peggy Lane – Cricket Lane – Ecclesfield.

Start: The Horseshoe at the junction of Shiregreen Lane and Bellhouse Road, Pismire Hill, Shiregreen. Map reference 371921.

Finish: The Travellers' Inn, Ecclesfield. Map reference 361940

Distance: 3½ miles.

Map: "Sheffield (North) and Stocksbridge", number 726 in the Ordnance Survey's "Pathfinder" series.

Public Transport: The start is served by bus number 47 from Flat Street in the city centre. Daily including Sundays. Ecclesfield has a choice of frequent bus services to the city centre, Meadowhall and Chapeltown.

By Car: The start may be reached by following the A6135 from the city centre. Parking at Concord Park. Ecclesfield is on the A6135 between Sheffield and Chapeltown. There is a car park in the village centre or at the Travellers'.

Refreshments: The Horseshoe and numerous pubs in Ecclesfield serve bar meals.

The Travellers' Inn

The Travellers' Inn stands at the junction of Green Lane and the Common in Ecclesfield, a prominent red-brick building. The large open bar is subdivided by mahogany and brass rail partitions and the decor is best described as Laura Ashley with Turkey carpets. One or two shelves display crockery and copperware and there is a selection of pictures. It is one of Tetley's Big Steak Pubs.

Tetley's Bitter on hand pump is always available, normally accompanied by a guest beer. On the day I called the offering was Davenport's Traditional Bitter. There is also a selection of lagers – Skol, Lowenbrau and Castlemaine all on draught along with draught wines. There is a wide range of bar meals available.

Opening Times: Mondays to Saturdays, 11.00 a.m. to 11.00 p.m.; Sundays, 12.00 a.m. to 3.00 p.m. and 7.00 p.m. to 10.30 p.m.

The Route

From the Horseshoe cross the busy road junction to Shiregreen Lane and pass through the impressive wrought iron gates at the entrance to Concord Park. There are some distinctive black and white timbered houses beyond the park boundary to your left.

Keppel's Column

Stay forward for some 200 yards along the tarmac driveway, passing well to the left of the Sports Centre and the hockey pitches. Subsequently, but to your left, is a series of tennis courts.

At the first T-junction go right, turning right again at a second junction within the space of a few yards. Even at this stage of the walk there is a most rewarding panoramic view embracing Wincobank Iron-Age Fort away to your right (see Walk 4) and Keppel's Column near Thorpe Hesley more or less directly ahead. Reaching a height of 115 feet this stone column was erected by the second Marquis of Rockingham, twice Prime Minister, to mark the acquittal of Admiral Keppel at a court martial in 1778.

Closer to hand there is a perspective of Tinsley, Meadowhall and a long stretch of the M1

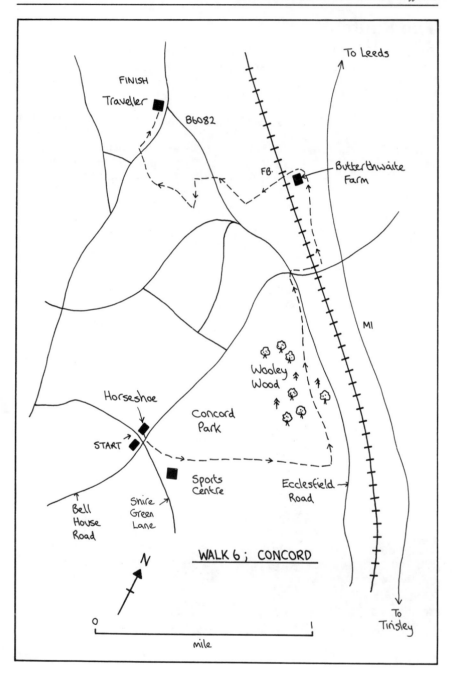

To Leeds

FINISH
Traveller

B6082

FB.

Butterthwaite Farm

M1

Wooley Wood

Horseshoe

Concord Park

START

Sports Centre

Ecclesfield Road

Bell House Road

Shire Green Lane

N

WALK 6 ; CONCORD

0   1

mile

To Tinsley

motorway as it heads south from the Tinsley Viaduct (see Walk 3). This vast area of Concord Park is occupied by several football pitches and a golf course.

On reaching a junction on the edge of the open space maintain direction to enter Woolley Wood. At the next intersection of paths, after approximately 100 yards, continue forwards to embark on the descent of a steep and stony path for about a quarter of a mile to another junction.

There turn left down a shallow flight of steps to another junction. Once again make a left turn and cross a footbridge constructed of railway sleepers before walking the level path through this ancient woodland.

Oak, sycamore and beech predominate but there are examples of hornbeam, once used in the manufacture of butchers' chopping blocks, and yew, famous for producing the long bows used to deadly effect by the archers of the English army during the medieval wars against France. Spring is the season for the bluebells, celandines, wild garlic and foxglove while for the bird-watching enthusiast there are chiffchaffs, wood warblers and greater spotted woodpecker.

On reaching a Y-junction fork right, soon making an exit onto Ecclesfield Road. Turn left along the pavement for a fine view of Thundercliffe Grange, a substantial square stone house. This strange name is a corruption of "Cindercliffe" or the "Heaps of Cinders" that were once produced by the local smelting industry.

After some 200 yards along the road, and by Neepsend Tools, turn right into Deep Lane which is signed to Thorpe Hesley. Pass under the railway bridge, walk over a stone bridge spanning the River Don and cross a disused railway level crossing.

Immediately before the M1 motorway, make a left turn into a signed bridleway known as Peggy Lane. Where this veers to the right and narrows, ignore a stile on your left and continue until Peggy Lane forms a junction with Butterthwaite Lane.

Turn left along this and, by the far end of Butterthwaite Farm, negotiate the stile on your left and strike out across the field to a conspicuous metal footbridge over the railway. At the far end continue over the stone footbridge spanning Blackburn Brook before turning right along the narrow path which hugs the left bank of the stream.

Stay with this clear path as it goes through a thin belt of trees and an enormous spread of rosebay willowherb to emerge onto a large open space of grass. Eventually it bends left to a footpath sign on Ecclesfield Road directly opposite to Woolley Wood Service Station.

Cross the road directly, and continue for 10 yards before crossing over Sicey Avenue to a footpath sign with an accompanying notice which reads, "Hartley Brook". Proceed over the open grassland of St. Michael's Field, passing to the left of a cricket ground. The path soon curves right behind some houses to meet an intersection in the path network.

Turn right over a small footbridge into Cricket Lane. This soon acquires a flagged surface as it climbs to Cross Hill where it meets the road opposite Peach Wilkinson, a firm of accountants.

Turn right down Cross Hill which soon develops into "The Common" keeping a sharp eye open for the cottage on your right which carries a plaque of Queen Victoria.

Descend the hill to the Travellers' Inn which stands on your left where "The Common" forms a junction with the A6135 to Barnsley and the B6082 to Wincobank.

Walk 7. Ecclesfield

A charming route through the rolling countryside of one of Sheffield's most ancient parishes with extensive vistas of the South Yorkshire landscape.

Route: Black Bull – Middleton Green – Whitley Woods – Wood End – Green Lane Farm – Elliott Lane – The Priory – Black Bull.

Start: The Black Bull, Church Street, Ecclesfield. Map reference 354942.

Distance: 3 miles.

Map: "Sheffield (North) and Stocksbridge", number 726 in the Ordnance Survey's "Pathfinder" series.

Public Transport: There are frequent buses daily including Sundays from Sheffield city centre, Meadowhall, Chapeltown and Barnsley.

By Car: The start is on the B6087 road which links the A61 at Grenoside with Chapeltown. There is limited parking in Priory Road alongside the parish church or in the public car park near the junction of Church Street and Town End Road.

Refreshments: There are several pubs in Ecclesfield which serve bar meals.

The Black Bull

With its impressive frontage the Black Bull stands facing Ecclesfield's ancient parish church. Passing through the front door you come face-to-face with a small central bar offering hand-drawn Tetley's Bitter, Guinness and cider.

To the left is a large games room while on the right is a spacious, comfortable lounge furnished in the modern fashion with a high ceiling. The walls are decorated with a collection of prints. Noticeably it is well patronised by the locals even though there are several other pubs within 100 yards. It does not offer bar meals although it is possible to buy crisps and similar snacks.

Opening Times: Mondays to Saturdays, 11.30 a.m. to 3.00 p.m. and 5.30 p.m. to 11.00 p.m.; Sundays 12.00 a.m. to 3.00 p.m. and 7.00 p.m. to 10.30 p.m.

The Black Bull

Ecclesfield

The name Ecclesfield is of Anglo-Saxon origin, probably meaning "Church Field" or "Church Clearing". Inside the present church there is the broken shaft and base of what is believed to be a Saxon cross which was used as a focal point for worship before the first church was built.

The village was mentioned in Domesday Book and traces of the first Norman Church may still be seen inside the present one which is chiefly the result of re-building work carried out in the fifteenth century.

At the Norman Conquest the parish, far more extensive than today, was given to the Benedictine monks of St. Wandrille's Abbey in Normandy and, in due course, they erected a small priory at Ecclesfield. This was never of any major significance; it had a chequered history and was suppressed by Henry VIII when the lands passed to the Earls of Talbot and, later, the Dukes of Norfolk.

The church, dedicated to St. Mary and often referred to as "The Minster of the Moors" because of its size, suffered damage during the Civil War when almost all of its stained glass windows was broken. It was restored to its present glory by the Reverend Alfred Gatty, Dean of

York, who was Vicar of Ecclesfield from 1839 to 1903. His wife, Margaret, enjoyed contemporary fame as the author of children's books, notably "Parables from Nature". Her father was chaplain to Nelson at Trafalgar and is buried in the churchyard. So, too, is Joseph Hunter whose research unearthed so much of the history of Sheffield and Hallamshire.

Perhaps the most unusual exhibits inside the church are the bugles, standards and swords of the Ecclesfield Parish Infantry, a volunteer corps raised in the village in 1804 when England lived in fear of an invasion by Napoleon's army. As this never materialised the volunteers saw no active services except to quell one or two local disturbances

The Route

From the front entrance of the Black Bull cross Church Street into the churchyard. Pass the village stocks before reaching the church itself where a left turn leads to the lych gate. Pass through onto Priory Road and cross directly onto a broad track which is signed as a footpath.

On your immediate left is the impressive stone hall, the Gatty Memorial, built in 1904 to mark the life and achievements of the Reverend Alfred Gatty, Vicar of Ecclesfield from 1839 to 1903 who is buried in the churchyard. So, too, is his daughter, Mrs. Ewing, who coined the name "Brownies" for the junior branch of the Girl Guide Movement.

Just beyond the hall negotiate a stone step stile before maintaining direction to the left of a wall and with the cemetery on your right. Pass through a small gate in the top corner of the field, climb a wooden stile and stay to the left of some wooden stables before starting an ascent of the field immediately to the left of a hawthorn hedge. Down below on your left are some houses while some distance away but directly ahead, is a view of Greno Woods. Closer to hand there is a magnificent spread of gorse.

Where the path curves round to the right look out for an unsigned path forking off down the slope on your left. Take this. Pass to the left of and just below another patch of gorse to a wooden stile set into a hedgerow.

Take your direction across the next field from the waymarker arrow fixed to the stile, aiming for a pylon in the far left-hand corner. By this turn left and pass between some houses to meet The Wheel. This is a lane which derives its name from the cobbled footpaths leading to the water-wheels which once powered the industries in the valley bottom.

Turn right along this lane for some 20 yards before forking right into

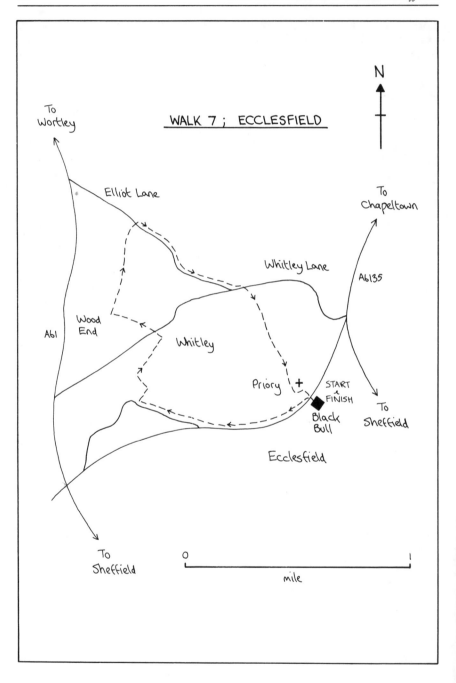

Cinderhill Lane. Initially this dips to pass Whitley Cricket ground on your right before climbing and then levelling out to pass the "Grenoside" village sign. Beyond is a row of houses known as Middleton Green which stand where the lane bends sharply to the left.

Immediately before the row of houses make a right turn onto an unsigned bridleway which has a tall hedge on the left and a view of Keppel's Column in the far distance to your right.

After 100 yards the track clings to the hedgerow as it makes a 90 degree turn to the left followed by another to the right. Beyond these turns it develops into a hedged lane lined with hedge parsley, purple loosestrife and other flowers.

The bridleway soon passes Oak Cottage and between other houses before making an exit onto Whitley Lane. Turn left to pass Sylvester's Farm, now advertising Meadow Fayre, and Whitley Hall farm. Both of these have mullioned widows which provide a clue to their seventeenth century origins.

Just beyond Barn House fork right into a lane signed as a footpath which has a wall on the right. After dipping slightly it climbs until reaching a small cluster of well maintained cottages known as "Wood End".

By the red telephone kiosk turn right into a metalled lane. After fewer than 100 yards, and where the lane bends sharply to the right as it approaches a five-barred gate in front of a house, fork left up a narrow path indicated by a waymark which is partially obscured by a rather luxuriant hedgerow.

Negotiate a wooden stile after 20 yards and cross the following field by keeping to the immediate left of a hedgerow to reach a stile in the field corner. Beyond this, continue losing height, still to the left of a hedge and following the field boundary as it curves. By a rusty five-barred metal gate on your right, veer right onto a broad track which stays along the edge of the field until passing Green Lane Farm on your right.

A very short distance beyond the farm negotiate a small stone step stile. Within five yards this is followed by a wooden stile. After a further 10 yards there is a type of squeezer stile which has been roughly fashioned out of a bedstead.

Through this climb steeply to the left of a wooden fence for approximately 60 yards to reach a stone step stile adjacent to a pylon. Then maintain direction over the next field to a stone step stile which provides an exit onto Elliot Lane.

Turn right to walk for half a mile along this quiet surfaced road as it loses altitude by the entrance to Whitley Hall, now a hotel, until it forms a junction with Whitley Lane. Turn left but, after 30 yards, take a signed lane on the right. After some 20 yards this lane curves to the right as it runs alongside a wooden fence on the left.

Where the fence terminates maintain direction across the field with another view of Keppel's Column away to your left and of the square tower of Ecclesfield Parish Church only a short distance ahead.

The path passes beneath overhead wires as it dips into the Brook valley where it becomes flagged. Cross the tiny footbridge before climbing for the short distance to a T-junction with footpath signs adjacent. There, turn left to meet the end of Priory Road. Continue along this until it meets Church Road and turn left for the few yards to the Black Bull.

Walk 8. Grenoside

A delightful walk especially in spring and early summer when bluebells, wild garlic and anemones carpet the ground. This route, although well within the boundaries of the City of Sheffield, is almost completely through mixed woodlands. The paths, for the most part, are wide but there is one long section which climbs quite steeply.

Route: Norfolk Arms, Grenoside — Greno Woods — Greno Knoll — The Norfolk Arms

Start: The Norfolk Arms, Penistone Road, Grenoside. Map reference 336943

Distance: 3 miles.

Map: "Sheffield (North) and Stocksbridge", number 726 in the Ordnance Survey's "Pathfinder" series

Public Transport: Buses 78, 80, 91, 98 and 238 from the city centre. Also frequent daily (including Sunday) buses from Huddersfield and Penistone.

By Car: The Norfolk Arms is on the A61 Sheffield to Barnsley road. There is a small parking space behind the Norfolk Arms accessible from Whitley Lane.

Refreshments: The Norfolk Arms serves bar meals at lunch time and in the evenings Mondays to Fridays.

The Norfolk Arms

One of several Norfolk Arms in Sheffield, showing the extensive influence of this important political family in the area, this one stands at the junction of Whitley Lane with Penistone Road in Grenoside to the north of the city. It is sturdily built in stone with a square appearance from the outside. Inside the L-shaped bar boasts a stone fireplace and a low ceiling complete with wooden beams.

The large picture frame window at the rear overlooks the beer garden and commands an almost breathtaking view over Ecclesfield as far as Keppel's Column at Thorpe Hesley beyond.

Landlord Alan Ward serves Ward's Best Bitter and won their Cellar Award in 1993, testimony indeed to the quality of his beer. In addition there is a range of lagers, wines and spirits. Bar meals are on offer at lunch times and in the evenings but only from Monday to Friday.

Opening Times: Mondays to Saturdays, 11.30 a.m. to 3.00 p.m. and 5.30 p.m. to 11.00 p.m.; Sundays 12.00 a.m. to 3.00 p.m. and 7.00 p.m. to 10.30 p.m.

The Norfolk Arms

The Route

On leaving the Norfolk Arms cross the busy A61 to enter the road opposite, Norfolk Hill. After 10 yards make a right turn over a wooden stile onto a signed path, so entering the mixed deciduous woodland almost at once.

For the first 250 yards the wide path climbs gently alongside a wire fence on the left to reach a footpath finger post at the northern end of Woodside Lane where there is a junction of several routes. Maintain direction for a further 10 yards to a second footpath sign. There make a right turn over a wooden stile to meet a Y-junction after a mere 25 yards. Fork right, soon passing to the left of an enormous metal pylon carrying overhead power lines, to reach a form of wooden squeezer stile located in a fence. Pass through this and turn right along a very broad track which has a stone wall on the left.

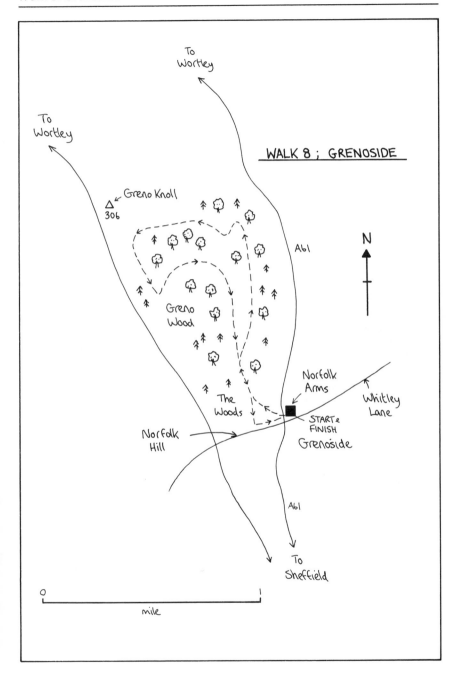

In spring and early summer this section of the woodland enjoys a symphony of birdsong provided by an orchestra of blackbirds, blue tits, great tits, coal tits, chaffinch, robins, wrens, tree creepers, thrushes and chiffchaff while the solos are provided by the greater spotted woodpecker.

After approximately 70 yards the broad track or bridleway arrives at another Y-junction. Fork right to enjoy a view to the east where thinning operations have opened-up a prospect of the countryside towards Wentworth and Hoober Stand. (see Walk 28).

At the subsequent Y-junction take the left hand path or bridleway. At week-ends you will meet frequent parties of horse riders also enjoying these woodlands. The route is now lined with heather and bilberry all the way until it emerges into a small clearing with a five-barred gate which leads to pasture lands on your right. There is also a very conspicuous Fountain Forestry notice about not disturbing felled timber. In this clearing make a right-angled left turn onto another bridleway which climbs a stony track to a T-junction. Turn right onto a broad track which climbs steeply for more than half a mile through the trees and spreads of bluebells until arriving at a T-junction. The Triangulation Pillar on Greno Knoll is only a short distance away to your right.

At this junction turn left to walk along the 300 metre contour with a broad, sandy track under your boots, all the time keeping a sharp eye open for the giant ant hills which are scattered along the route. At this height, the deciduous trees have been joined by conifers while several patches of gorse add variety to the colour.

Continue until the track begins to lose height over a considerable distance to a small clearing with a T-junction. Turn right, eventually arriving at an inverted Y-junction.

Stay forward along the level sandy path which provides for some excellent, easy walking. Pass through a wooden squeezer stile adjacent to a five-barred gate and advance a further 15 yards to a second wooden squeezer stile which affords access to an intersection in the path network.

Make a left turn to an inverted Y-junction. Continue forward with a small stone wall on your right for approximately 100 yards before veering left through a break in the fence to pass a small pond formed by a walled spring on your left.

At the next Y-junction fork right to reach a wooden stile with a footpath sign alongside. Turn right into Woodside Lane, pass between the cottages and houses to meet Norfolk Hill. Turn left for the final 150 yards back to the Norfolk Arms.

Walk 9. Wortley

An undulating excursion through lush pastoral countryside which forms part of the Wharncliffe estate. It follows field paths and bridleways and includes some undemanding climbing.

Route: Wortley Arms – Finkle Street Lane – Rough Lane – Wharncliffe Reservoir – Booth Wood – Howbrook Lane – Wortley Park – Wortley Arms

Start: Wortley Arms, Wortley village. Map reference 307994

Distance: 3¼ miles.

Map: "Sheffield (North) and Stocksbridge", number 726 in the Ordnance Survey's "Pathfinder" series.

Public Transport: Wortley has frequent daily services from Sheffield, Huddersfield, Meadowhall (not Sundays) and Barnsley. (not Sundays).

By Car: Wortley is on the A629 Sheffield to Huddersfield road. There is limited parking off the main road by the Post Office.

Refreshments: The Wortley Arms serves bar meals at lunch time and in the evenings. There is also a cafe in the village which opens from 10.00 a.m. to 5.00 p.m. on Thursdays, Fridays, Saturdays and Sundays.

The Wortley Arms

The Wortley Arms is located on a very acute bend in the A629 facing the parish church. As the front door opens directly onto the main road it is safer to enter the pub through the car park.

Once installed, however, there is a very cosy and welcoming atmosphere created by the wood panelled walls and thick beams. The large stone fireplace boasts an old-fashioned grid-iron while one unplastered area of stonework has the coat-of-arms of the Earls of Wharncliffe inset into it. The lights are suspended on a horizontal cartwheel and, as might be expected, there is a scattering of copper, brass and pewter ware.

Landlord Barry Hulme serves Stone's Best Bitter, Younger's IPA and Courage's Director's but pride of place must go to the Earl's Ale which is brewed in the cellar under the floor.

Opening Times: Mondays to Saturdays 11.30 a.m. to 3.00 p.m. and 5.30 p.m. to 11.00 p.m.; Sundays 12.00 a.m. to 3.00 p.m. and 7.00 p.m. to 10.30 p.m.

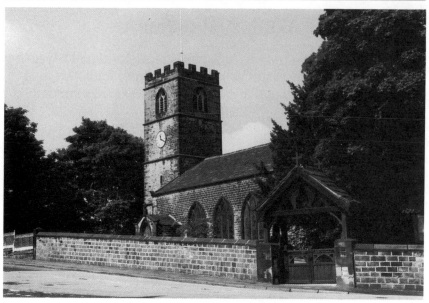

The church at Wortley

Wortley

Excavations on Wharncliffe Chase have revealed the presence of a small British settlement there during the Roman period but there is little evidence of direct Roman influence in the area.

The name "Wharncliffe" derives from the Scandinavian word meaning "Quern-Cliff" while Wortley stems from the Anglo-Saxon for "a clearing used for growing vegetables". The village received a mention in the Domesday Book of 1087 and even two hundred years later was far larger than nearby Penistone, a situation now dramatically reversed.

It is claimed that the iron industry was brought to the parish by Cistercian monks in the thirteenth century. Certainly, arrow heads forged there were used against the French armies during the Battle of Crecy in 1346 and the Battle of Agincourt in 1415. This concentration on armaments continued until well into the seventeenth century when Wortley supplied canon balls to the Royalist army of King Charles I during the English Civil War. By the nineteenth century, however, a transformation to more peaceful products had been made with railway lines and axles for locomotives and carriages emerging from the Wortley forges which had long enjoyed a high reputation for fashioning high quality nails.

The first mention of a church at Wortley occurs in 1268 when it is believed that a chapel-of-ease within the parish of Tankersley existed there. It did not become a parish in its own right until 1746. There have been several additions and alterations to the church fabric, the last being a completely new roof following a disastrous fire in 1946.

The most notable memorial is that of Edward Wortley whose wife, Lady Mary Wortley Montague, returned from Turkey with the idea of using vaccination as a cure for smallpox.

Wortley Hall, which is not open to the public, is the home of the Earls of Wharncliffe. Wortley was the birthplace of William Nevinson, a highwayman who actually rode from London to York in the space of 15 hours, a feat erroneously attributed to Dick Turpin and one which earned him the soubriquet of "Swift Nicks Nevinson" from no less an admirer than King Charles 11. However, despite this royal favour, he finally paid the ultimate penalty of all such brigands.

The Route

Exercising extreme caution, because this is a busy main road and the pub is located in the middle of a very acute Z-bend, leave the Wortley Arms car park by turning left to walk along the A629 in the direction of Sheffield. After 20 yards, turn right into a covered and flagged passageway in the middle of a row of white cottages. There is no footpath sign to announce its existence.

Emerge by a short flight of steps into a large field. Descend close to the stone wall on your right, over which is the churchyard. Ahead there is a view of Wharncliffe Crags. Where the path meets a track at the bottom of the field stay forward with a playing field having replaced the churchyard on your right.

Within yards, a large metal gate provides an exit onto Finkle Street Lane. Cross slightly to the right, negotiate a stone step stile and then take your direction from the arm of the footpath finger post.

The path continues losing height until, having crossed a tiny stream, it reaches another step stile. Beyond this maintain direction, with Sycamore Farm on your right, to a wooden stile alongside a five-barred gate.

Staying to the left of a row of cottages, cross a small bridge to a second wooden stile adjacent to a cattle grid. Continue under the tunnel which carries the A616 overhead and then immediately make a left turn over a wooden stile with a footpath finger post.

Follow the wide track which initially runs parallel with the A616.

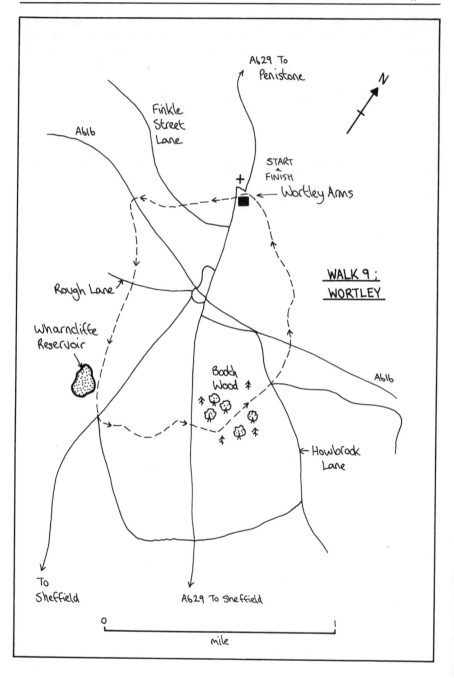

After 100 yards and having crossed a stream which is fenced-off by some wooden railings, curve right to embark on a long climb which takes you beneath two sets of overhead wires.

In doing so veer very gradually towards the left-hand corner of the field, negotiate a waymarked stone step stile and stay to the right of a stone wall until another stile brings you to Rough Lane.

Cross directly to another stile with footpath post and maintain direction along a slightly raised grass terrace which runs along the left-hand side of a long narrow field.

There is a small abandoned quarry on your left while Moorside Farm is visible away to your right. It is a rolling, pastoral and well wooded landscape with nesting lapwing in early summer.

Pass through a gap in a derelict wall to a waymarked stile which apparently has no reason for existing. Continue to the right of a stone wall until gaining a stile in the far corner of the field with a wood immediately in front. Turn left over the stile and then right before crossing a track to a waymarked stone step stile.

Maintain direction with Wharncliffe Reservoir, although not visible, just over the wall on your right. Several notices proclaim that this is private property and forbids walkers and sightseers to enter.

Beyond the next stile, veer diagonally left towards an obvious footpath sign alongside a stone step stile which provides an exit onto Woodhead Road. Cross directly into the facing minor road signed to Howbrook.

However, after 50 yards turn left by another footpath sign to follow the path along the edge of the field with a wall on your right. From this vantage point you are able to enjoy wide ranging views of South Yorkshire towards Barnsley, Rotherham, Doncaster and Sheffield. On a clear day they extend much further.

Cundy Houses, a short distance away to your left, are soon passed and, shortly afterwards, you are opposite Carlton House, a typical sturdy Yorkshire stone affair. 60 yards beyond a gateway turn right over a stone step stile in the wall and then turn immediately to the left for some 50 yards to the corner of the field.

There turn right with hawthorns and other trees forming a line on your left. At this point the path is far from distinct but remain along the field boundary.

By a solitary gatepost at the end of a short stretch of wall veer left towards a large compost heap. Usually, when the grass is long, the farmer drives his tractor along the line of the path so that it is easy to follow. From the compost heap bear right along a track and pass beneath overhead wires to reach the A629. Cross to the footpath sign opposite which has a stone step stile adjacent.

The new path loses height to the right of Booth Wood with a line of electricity wires running parallel. At the bottom of the slope, enter the wood which is a rich mixture of broadleaved trees including oak, hazel, sycamore and ash. The ground flora includes a magnificent spread of bluebells in spring but there are also nettles, brambles, ivy, wild garlic and rosebay willowherb. These woodlands resound to the songs of blackbird, blackcap, thrush, robin, chaffinch and numerous other species including greater spotted woodpecker.

After crossing a small stream which has a distinctly trilling sound, the path climbs for a short distance before emerging from the wood. Stay to the immediate right of the woodland boundary and, by the corner of the wood maintain your line of direction across a field to a wooden stile standing waif-like and forlorn with no apparent use now that the hedgerow has been grubbed out to comply with the demands of modern agricultural techniques.

Continue along the same line of direction to the right of a barbed wire fence before reaching a wooden stile and Howbrook Lane. Cross into Peatfields Lane but, after a mere 10 yards, turn left over a rather obscured stone step stile with a footpath sign and an ivy-clad tree close by. Aim for the diagonally opposite right-hand corner of the field where there is a wooden stile.

Descend the flight of steps and, taking care, cross the busy A616 before climbing a second flight of steps. Pass through an old wooden kissing gate into Copley Wood.

After only a very short distance exit the woods by a wooden stile. Turn left to follow the field boundary for 100 yards. There turn right along another field boundary to a stile adjacent to a four-barred gate.

Over the stile turn left along the wide track which runs through Wortley Park with the Hall away to your right. Pass to the left of Park Lodge and keep forward until reaching the centre of the village and the A629 by the post office. Turn left for the Wortley Arms.

Walk 10. Green Moor

A varied route through riverside woodlands and over upland pastures using a mixture of footpaths and bridleways. There are several stretches of gentle climbing with one short steep section.

Route: Finkle Street Lane — Tin Mill Dam — White Carr Head — Low Lathe — Old Park House — Park Lane — Hunshelf Bank — Green Moor — Holly Lane — Finkle Street

Start: The junction of the B6088 with the minor road to Thurgoland and by a disused railway bridge. Map reference 299993.

Distance: 4½ miles.

Map: "Sheffield (North) and Stocksbridge", number 726 in the Ordnance Survey's "Pathfinder" series.

Public Transport: The start is served by daily buses from Barnsley and Stocksbridge. There is a less frequent daily service from Barnsley and Stocksbridge to Green Moor.

By Car: The start is reached from either Stocksbridge or Wortley by using the B6088, or from Thurgoland by using a minor road. There is a small lay-by for parking.

Refreshments: The Rock pub in Green Moor serves bar meals at lunch time and in the evenings except Sundays.

The Rock

The Rock at Green Moor is appropriately named because it stands on the floor of a former quarry with the stone walls rising all around. Built of millstone grit to serve as the wages office, it is more than 200 years old. For about 130 of those years it has served as a pub and once incorporated the village shop.

It now has two rooms, their distinguishing feature being the tongue and groove ceilings which are painted white between the wooden beams. The stone-fronted bar and the wooden backed settles all contribute to the cosy country atmosphere. There is a children's playground and for adults seeking relaxation there is a pool room.

Landlord Mat Monfredi extends a warm welcome to ramblers at this family-run hostelry and the hungry walker will be strongly tempted by the wide range of bar meals available every lunch time and every evening except Sunday.

The thirsty may slake their thirst with a choice from Stone's Best Bitter, John Smith's Bitter and Bass, all cask-conditioned plus a selection of lagers including Carling Black Label.

Opening Times: Mondays to Saturdays, 11.00 a.m. to 11.00 p.m.; Sundays 12.00 a.m. to 3.00 p.m. and 7.00 p.m. to 10.30 p.m.

Green Moor

Situated on the high plateau overlooking the River Don in its infant stages, this tiny upland settlement of Green Moor once enjoyed a national reputation for the quality of its Millstone Grit known as Green Moor Delph. Highly prized as a paving stone, it was used for the footpaths surrounding Sheffield Town Hall. Today, the quarry is defunct and Green Moor is principally a farming community boosted by commuters from Sheffield.

By the entrance to the car park of the Rock is the Green Moor village pump. First brought into use in 1909, it was restored to full working order by local volunteers in 1984.

The well at Greenmoor

During the Second World War and for a few years afterwards there was a simple Youth Hostel at Green Moor which was extremely popular with walkers and cyclists from all parts of South Yorkshire.

The Route

From the road junction walk a few yards in the direction of Stocksbridge before turning right down a flight of concrete steps onto a signed path which crosses a field to a cul-de-sac which forms the approach to a row of cottages.

Cross this to a small wooden gate and maintain direction for a further 75 yards to cross a large metal footbridge spanning the River Don. For the more adventurous there is a set of stepping stones. At the far end of the bridge turn right along the clear riverside path as it passes through deciduous woodlands where blue bells are rampant in May.

Having passed between two waymarked gateposts Tin Mill Dam, a favoured haunt of local anglers, is reached on your left. Continue along the lane and pass through a gateway with a stile alongside to emerge onto a road.

Turn right, and using the grass verge, walk for 75 yards before making another right turn into a surfaced lane signed as a footpath. This climbs steeply towards a set of pylons. By the first pylon, swing right and, still climbing, enjoy a superb view down the Don valley as the river flows from the moorlands towards Sheffield city centre.

At the Y-junction by a forest of pylons fork right to climb the track which passes between the buildings at Low Lathe Farm to a T-junction.

Turn left to meet a surfaced lane after 100 yards. Maintain direction to Old Park House, a solid stone house obviously built by someone looking for a little prestige. By the house, fork right towards the barn and, staying to the left of this, follow the unsurfaced lane which, at the far end, swings right for ten yards and then curves left before hugging the contour below Hunshelf Bank.

It is flanked with hawthorn, rowan and holly while the slope on your right is speckled with gorse, heather and bilberry. To the left you look down onto the modernised Stocksbridge Steelworks, a far cry from the old major factories once found between Rotherham and Sheffield. Beyond is the small town of Stocksbridge which stands almost entirely on one slope of the valley with the conspicuous moorland church of Bolsterstone visible in the far distance.

The lane, shown as Park Lane on the maps, becomes walled and is accompanied on either side by overhead wires. After almost a mile pass

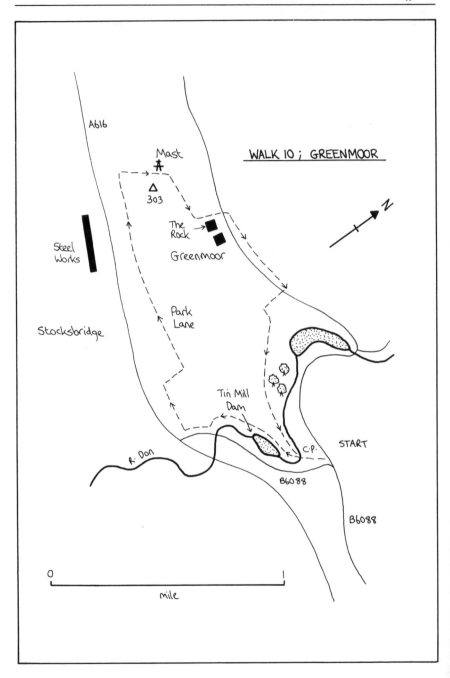

WALK 10 ; GREENMOOR

through a squeezer stile adjacent to a rusty five-barred gate to approach Well House Farm. Keeping this on your left, continue for a further 200 yards until meeting the driveway to Well House Cottage and two footpath signs, one on either side of the lane.

Turn right through a squeezer stile to meet a Y-junction almost at once. Take the left-hand path, climbing directly up the hillside through the gorse and beneath overhead wires. Where the path becomes indistinct, maintain direction by aiming for the Cellnet Communications Tower on the summit.

On meeting the corner of a stone wall, stay forward to walk between it and the main communication tower. A short distance away to your right is the Triangulation Pillar on Hunshelf bank at 303 metres. Ahead is an extensive panorama towards Barnsley.

From the Cellnet installation a track descends the slope, passing to the left of Hill Top Farm before meeting a T-junction. Turn right along the lane for several hundred yards but by a stone bungalow, "The Willows", and the 30 MPH signs turn left down a short side road which leads to the main street through Green Moor village.

Turn right to pass to the left of the old Board School, erected in 1879 but now no longer serving its original purpose. Just beyond, and also on your right, is The Rock. Continue beyond the pub as Green Moor Road becomes Well Hill. Ignore the first footpath on your right but, about 150 yards beyond the Green Moor village sign and by a substantial stone house, turn right into Holly Hall Lane which affords some fine views towards Wortley with its unmistakeable church tower.

The next piece of navigation requires very careful observation. Pass between two gateposts without a gate and 40 yards beyond, where the lane bends round to the left, there is the dead stump of a tree bearing a yellow waymark. Ignore the first stile on your left. Proceed a further 10 yards and, where the lane curves round to the right, go left over another waymarked stone stile by a holly tree.

Proceed to the left of a fence and then continue along a grass terrace with holly and hawthorn trees before negotiating a waymarked stone step stile in the apex of a small triangular field. Stay forward. The delightful grassy path skirts the boundary of Forge Rocher Woods as it crosses the lower edge of a sloping field and continues through an avenue of trees. This is countryside walking at its finest.

After going between two gateposts descend to a wooden stile to enter woodlands. The path widens, losing height more quickly as it becomes a track. At the T-junction in the valley bottom re-join your outward route by turning left for the final 300 yards to your starting point.

Walk 11. Loxley Common

Starting from the Supertram in Middlewood, this route climbs steeply through the outer suburbs before continuing to even greater heights along well defined footpaths across Loxley Common. The effort is rewarded with panoramic views over the northern areas of the city and beyond.

Route: Middlewood—Langsett Avenue—Rural Lane—Loxley Edge—Loxley Common — Bower Plantation — Rowel Cottage — Stour Lane — Langsett Avenue — Middlewood

Start: Supertram stop at the junction of Langsett Avenue with Middlewood Road (A6102). Map reference 326912.

Distance: 3½ miles.

Map: 1."Sheffield (North) and Stocksbridge", number 726 in the Ordnance Survey's "Pathfinder" series. 2. "A to Z" Street Atlas of Sheffield.

Public Transport: The start is served by frequent daily buses from the city centre (Pond Street Interchange) and Stocksbridge. It will also be served by Supertram when the network is completed.

By Car: The start may be reached by travelling from the city centre along the A61 and then taking the A6012. There is some parking in side streets. People travelling by car may reduce the amount of street walking by using the car park on Rural or Rowell Lane at map reference 319908 reached by driving up Langsett Avenue.

Refreshments: The Rose and Crown serves bar meals at lunch times and in the evenings.

The Rose And Crown

Along with several other properties in this area the Rose and Crown is stone built. Its age is unknown but its antiquity is revealed by the thickness of its walls and deep-set windows. For centuries it has been the meeting place for the Wadsley and Loxley Commoners who govern the grazing lands over which this route passes.

The lower bar area has always been a pub but the section up the short flight of four steps used for bar meals and as a small restaurant, has been converted from three adjoining cottages. This old-worlde atmosphere is maintained by wooden-backed settles along with displays of porcelain cats, pigs, ancient electric irons and hunting horns. The ceiling has impressively thick wooden beams. Landlord Colin Westhead serves cask-conditioned Tetley's Bitter and Stone's Best Bitter.

Opening Times: Mondays to Saturdays 11.30 a.m. to 2.30 p.m. and 6.30 p.m. to 11.00 p.m.; Sundays 12.00 a.m. to 3.00 p.m. and 7.00 p.m. to 10.30 p.m.

The Rose and Crown

Loxley Commons

Loxley Common, a steep rocky slope below Loxley Edge, lies on a sandstone ridge to the north west of Sheffield. The last three letters of the name, "ley" mean "forest clearing", the forest originally consisting of oak and birch. These were cleared many centuries ago to allow for the grazing of sheep and cattle which, in turn resulted in the appearance of heather moorland.

Since grazing came to an end, birch and bracken are becoming dominant and, as a result of several fires during the 1970s, much of the heather has been replaced by grass and even more bracken. Today the area is managed by the Sheffield City Council's Countryside Department which has also created a number of new footpaths and bridleways.

From time immemorial the local villagers enjoyed the right of grazing their animals on the Commons but in the early nineteenth century the Commons were divided between the landowners who erected boundary walls, the remnants of which may still be traced during the course of this walk.

Another unusual feature of Loxley Common is the presence of Ganister, a form of silica rock used in the manufacture of firebricks. These were used to line the furnaces of the Sheffield steel industry.

Coal was discovered near the surface and was extracted from the eighteenth century by digging drift mines. Most of the traces of these workings have long since vanished but there are several small abandoned quarries from which sandstone was taken for house building.

In 1782 a local jeweller, Nathan Andrews, was murdered on Loxley Common by Frank Fearn who was subsequently arrested and executed. Afterwards, his corpse was exhibited on a gibbet on Loxley Edge, remaining there until it fell down in 1797.

The post was left where it stood until 1810 when, according to a local tradition, it was cut down to provide a footbridge over the River Loxley. It was washed away in the great flood of 1864 but, after being salvaged, was incorporated into the building of a row of cottages.

The Route

Alighting from the Supertram, turn into Langsett Avenue and proceed up the straight, steep climb for approximately half a mile. This is one of the steepest sections of all the walks in this book and is equal to many you will find in the Peak District. The only difference is that your route is lined with houses.

On reaching Worrall Road cross directly into Well Lane, a very narrow thoroughfare which continues uphill for approximately a further 100 yards before meeting Rural Lane.

Turn right along this for 150 yards and then turn left into the car park. From the entrance proceed in a straight line to the through stile adjacent to a wooden five-barred gate. Proceed along the stony path as it ascends gently through rosebay willowherb, bramble, sycamore, heather, bilberry and gorse until emerging onto a level plateau.

This was the site of the former Wadsley Common Playing Fields which are no longer used but where the former mowing regime has produced a carpet of wavy hairgrass which is currently being colonised

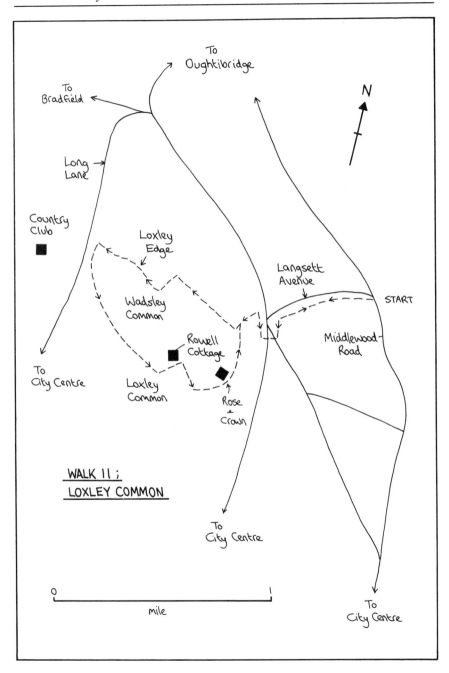

To
Oughtibridge

To
Bradfield

N

Long
Lane

Country
Club

Loxley
Edge

Langsett
Avenue

START

Wadsley
Common

Middlewood
Road

To
City Centre

Rowell
Cottage

Loxley
Common

Rose
Crown

WALK 11 ;
LOXLEY COMMON

To
City Centre

0   1
mile

To
City Centre

by birch and oak. It is a site favoured by hovering kestrels hawking for field mice and voles.

At the first Y-junction fork right, climbing again until reaching a T-junction. Turn left for a spell of level walking through a carpet of heather and bracken until reaching another T-junction after 100 yards.

Make a right turn to walk through silver birch and more gorse and heather. At the next intersection of paths maintain direction, ignoring attractive-looking paths to both left and right.

Continue to the right of a crumbling stone wall, one of several built after the enclosure of the Commons during the nineteenth century and which now provides a perfect habitat for weasels which may often be seen in the vicinity.

On your immediate right is Hillsborough Golf Course. The path eventually levels as it enters an area of scrub consisting mainly of birch with more enclosure walls. Negotiate a through stile to enter an area of heath land which is rather reminiscent of parts of Dorset and the New Forest, somewhat surprising since this is so close to the centre of Sheffield.

At the subsequent T-junction, turn right to pass a solitary stone gatepost lying on its side and making a very useful seat. The path, now very well maintained, negotiates a wooden barrier to another T-junction. Turn right again but now with a view of the Peak District moors away to your left.

Pass through a wooden squeezer stile with a galvanised gate alongside before walking through another car park on Loxley Edge at some 239 metres above sea level.

Beyond the car park, continue along the wide track for 100 yards to a three-armed footpath post which stands by a gateway without gates some few yards from Long Lane. By the footpath post turn left along a bridleway and, with Loxley Country Club on the far side of Long Lane, start losing height to a Y-junction.

Fork left through birch woodland where ragwort in abundance flanks the path. At the next T-junction turn left but, by a large boulder, swing to the right to have the occasional field appearing to your right

At an intersection in the path network, by a telegraph pole, maintain direction to pass Rowell Cottage before arriving at a wooden kissing gate by a footpath sign.

Through the gate continue forwards along a wide track until reaching a junction by a facing metal five-barred gate which carries a notice which reads, "Private Land. No Entry". As this effectively bars all forward progress, turn right and walk 150 yards to a twin-armed footpath post by a T-junction.

Make a left turn onto another wide track, soon passing Loxley House Farm, a fine stone building with a stone roof which stands on your right. A short distance beyond, some modern red-brick houses appear on your left and the track acquires a surface. By the next footpath sign turn left into Bland Lane, an area which is a curious blend of old stone cottages and recently-built brick houses.

At the far end of Bland Lane make a right turn into Aldene Road but, by Holly Beech Farm, turn left into Luke Lane to reach the Rose and Crown. Suitably refreshed, turn left out of the pub, pass the car park and stay forward along the track which is, in fact, a continuation of Luke Lane.

By a footpath finger post, swing left and then, within a few yards and by a wire fence, swing right to walk between a fence on your left and a wall on your right to reach a wooden stile. Immediately beyond this turn right along your outward route to the car park.

Cross this to the entrance and turn right for 150 yards before turning left into Well Lane. Where this ends continue down Langsett Avenue back to the tram or bus stop on Middlewood Road.

Walk 12. Malin Bridge

An exploration of the countryside around the Loxley Valley using bridleways, field and woodland paths, many of which were created by workers on their way to the forges during the early days of the Industrial Revolution.

Route: Malin Bridge — Rivelin Valley — Myers Grove Lane — Greaves Lane — Robin Hood — Acorn Hill — Rowel Bridge — Olive Paper Mill — Low Matlock Lane — Wisewood — Malin Bridge

Start: The junction of Rivelin Valley Road and Holme Lane, Malin Bridge. Map reference 325894.

Distance: 4¼ miles.

Map: "Sheffield", number 743 in the Ordnance Survey's "Pathfinder" series.

Public Transport: Frequent buses to Malin Bridge from the Sheffield Interchange (Pond Street). Supertram from the City Centre.

By Car: From the City Centre follow the signs to Malin Bridge. From Manchester and the West leave the Snake Road (A57) at Rivelin Post Office to follow Rivelin Valley Road to Malin Bridge. There is no car park at Malin Bridge. Use the car park at Walkley Tilt, approximately a quarter of a mile along Rivelin Valley Road from Malin Bridge.

Refreshments: The Robin Hood serves bar meals.

The Robin Hood

The Robin Hood was built by a vicar in 1804 as a place of refreshment serving teas and cakes. He was also responsible for landscaping the surrounding area and creating walks through the woodland, hence the name of Little Matlock after the famous spa town in the Peak District.

After passing through the main entrance take the first door on the right to enter one of the two bars and it is like stepping into Robin's wild wood. It is filled with stags' heads, stuffed foxes, stoats, weasels, badgers, pheasants, capercaillies, owls and other forms of flesh and feathers. Even the sets of plates on display echo this wildlife theme with hunting scenes and sporting dogs. The bar is lined with wooden-backed settles while the good old-fashioned wooden tables are surrounded by stools. With its thick oak beams and coaching lamps it is pervaded by a genuine atmosphere of yester-year. Landlady Joan Laing serves

Stone's Best Bitter and Bass along with at least one guest brew which was Theakston's "Black Sheep" when I called. Bar snacks are served at both lunch-time and in the evenings. **Opening Times:** Mondays to Saturdays, 11.30 a.m. to 3.00 p.m. and 7.00 p.m. to 11.00 p.m.; Sundays, 12.00 a.m. to 3.00 p.m. and 7.00 p.m. to 10.30 p.m.

The Robin Hood

The Loxley Valley

The Loxley Valley is a fascinating mixture of natural woodlands, landscaped features and the remnants of an industrial past. The presence of Yellow Archangel, Dog's Mercury and other plants confirms that some of the woodlands, especially in the steeper cloughs, have never been touched by the hand of man but a large area of land around the Robin Hood is known to have been planted with oak, beech and elm plus exotic foreign imports approximately 150 years ago. All this has had an impact on the wildlife, increasing the number of bird species to be seen within the valley and the surrounding farmland. Great spotted woodpecker, jay, chaffinch, willow warbler, blue tits, great tits, wrens, blackbirds and thrushes are common species but in summer the blackcap, chiffchaff, and willow warbler add their songs to the dawn chorus.

This sylvan paradise became the focus of industrial activity from about 1500 when the waters of the River Loxley were harnessed to drive the water wheels which powered the small cutler's workshops and forges which laid the foundations of Sheffield's future greatness. By 1800 the two-mile stretch of river supported no fewer than 18 water wheels, each with its small dammed pond. Apart from its cutlers grinding their knives, the valley also supported factories producing paper, glass, and cloth or mills grinding corn, crushing clay or rolling wire.

In 1864 the collapse of the wall of Dale Dyke Dam sent an enormous wall of water down the valley, destroying everything in its path and causing no fewer than 250 deaths. Compensation payments made afterwards helped to modernise the industries along the Loxley and it is the remains of these that can seen along the this particular route. In particular there are the dams of Rowel Bridge Mill, the Olive Paper Mill, the Wisewood Forge and the Little Matlock Wheel. In addition, the valley also supported coal mining and the extraction of Ganister employed for the manufacture of fire bricks for lining the steel furnaces.

The Route

Start this walk at the junction of Stannington Road with Holme Lane and Rivelin Valley Road at Malin Bridge where the River Loxley joins the Rivelin.

By looking over the parapet of the bridge it is still possible to see the water wheel of the former Malin Bridge Corn Mill where a nature reserve is now in process of being established. It is incredible what can be achieved in inner city areas.

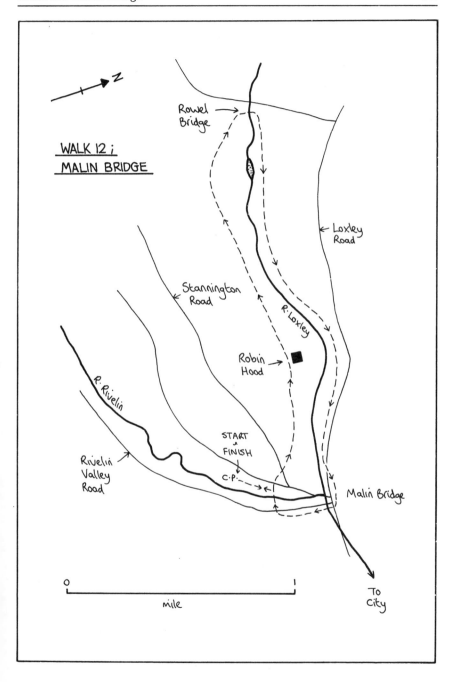

Walk along Rivelin Valley Road for approximately 250 yards, passing the fire station on the way. By a bridleway sign, turn right over a stone bridge spanning the River Rivelin and follow the track to Mousehole Forge, now a private residence.

For those arriving by car, leave the Walkley Tilt car park by turning right along the signed footpath through the trees with the River Rivelin on your right. Turn left over a plank footbridge and pass to the right of a sluice before meeting a bridleway by a stone bridge. Turn left to reach Mousehole Forge. Just beyond the Forge, at the Y-junction, veer left along another bridleway leading to Stannington Road opposite to The Anvil pub which serves John Smith's.

Cross the road and, keeping the pub on your left, enter Wood Lane. After a mere 50 yards make a right turn into Myers Grove Lane, recognised by a stained glass factory on the corner.

You will soon pass a renovated white house on your right which displays a weather vane in the form of a witch. A short distance beyond the Pines Grove Country Club, also on your right, fork right into Greaves Lane.

Pass a school on your left and continue climbing gradually with ever-widening views until, after half a mile, you reach the Robin Hood. Several paths form a junction at this point. Advance to the left of the pub before cornering round the back to join a signed bridleway. After 50 yards along this turn right over a wooden stile with a footpath finger post adjacent, to walk a delightfully level path through mixed deciduous woodlands on Acorn Hill.

These have established themselves since the hillside was cleared by felling during the First World War. The principal species are sycamore, ash, elm and oak with an under-storey of hazel, hawthorn and holly. in common with most elms those here have suffered severely through Dutch Elm Disease.

After half a mile through the woods fork left at a waymarked junction, the new path initially maintaining its height along the contour before climbing through the woods which in May are carpeted with bluebells.

Soon a stepped section carries you even higher and, at the top, swings right to another Y-junction. This time fork right to descend a stepped stretch of path. At the bottom turn left through a waymarked stile to cross a plank bridge to a ladder stile which provides an exit from the woodlands.

Advance to the immediate left of a wall-cum-fence across the bottom of a field to a through stile in the far corner. Continue in the same direction with the wall-cum-fence still on your right while enjoying a fine view of the Peak District moorlands in the far distance ahead. This is matched by the attractive pastoral prospect in the direction of Dungworth village to the right.

After 50 yards pass through a small gate and turn right onto a flagged path leading diagonally left down a meadow where sweet vernal grass, tormentil, mouse-eared-hawkweed and similar plants flourish and where the brown butterfly thrives.

Negotiate another small gate before turning right to pass beneath overhead power lines to a squeezer stile. Beyond this follow the cobbled footpath which descends steeply to the right of a stone wall to a wooden kissing gate with a three-armed footpath post adjacent. Turn right down the stepped path to Rowell Bridge before following the walled path to Rowell Lane.

Very little evidence remains of the former grinding workshops which once occupied this site, except for two wheel pits of the former water wheels used for driving the machinery.

Turn right along the road for 50 yards before making another right turn through a small gate with a three-armed footpath sign alongside. The first section of this route has been upgraded by Sheffield City Council's Countryside Department for use by disabled people and was officially opened by David Blunkett, M.P. in 1985 when he was Chairman of the City Council.

Follow this path with the River Loxley on the right and a splendid-looking Loxley Grange a short distance away to the left. Cross a goit by a small footbridge, staying forward until reaching Olive Mill Dam.

Keep this on your left and, having passed through a squeezer stile, continue to the far end of the former Olive Paper Mill. There pass through a wall gap and descend six steps onto a narrow path.

Cross the end of the leat by a set of stepping stones as the main path keeps the river on its right before turning left up another flight of steps to a through stile which allows an exit onto Black Lane. Turn right along this walled lane which is fringed with umbellifers and rowan and where a variety of birds are to be heard in spring.

Pass a row of cottages on your right. Shortly afterwards, where the lane bends through 90 degrees to the left to a T-junction, make a right turn into Little Matlock Lane. Look out for Little Matlock Wheel on your right close to a red brick chimney. A short path from the lane permits a closer examination.

Stay with Little Matlock Lane until, about 100 yards beyond a square stone house and by Riverside Motors, a Y-junction is reached. Take the path signed to Loxley Bottoms and Malin Bridge, descending a flight of 12 steps before crossing the silted-up site of the former dam for Broomhead Wheel.

After a quarter of a mile, by the next waymarked post, turn right down more steps towards a weir. Wisewood Forge Dam is on your left. Cross the metal footbridge by the ruined mill and stay forward along the main path until it meets Loxley Road. Turn right. After 50 yards make a right turn into Holme Lane where you will find your starting point.

If you are returning to your car at Walkley Tilt follow the instructions at the start of the walk until reaching the stone bridge over the River Rivelin where you will re-join your outward route.

Walk 13. The Rivelin

A steep climb through woodlands leads to an undulating ridge walk offering some outstanding views of the city and countryside. This is followed by a pleasant and undemanding riverside saunter.

Route: Rivelin Post Office – The Coppice – Blackbrook Wood – Bell Hagg – Samehill Farm – Rivelin Valley – Rivelin Post Office

Start: Rivelin Post Office at the junction of the A57 (Snake Road) with Rivelin Valley Road. Map reference 289872.

Distance: 4 miles.

Map: "Sheffield", number 743 in the Ordnance Survey's "Pathfinder" series.

Public Transport: Frequent daily buses from Sheffield Interchange (Pond Street).

By Car: Rivelin Valley Post Office may be reached by using the A57 and following the signs to Glossop from Sheffield City Centre. From Manchester, follow the A57. There is a car park off Rails Road, about one minute's walk from the Rivelin Post Office.

Refreshments: The Bell Hagg serves bar meals at lunch time and in the evenings. Beverages, soft drinks, sandwiches and light snacks are available from the Rivelin Valley Post Office.

The Bell Hagg

This unusual pub name appears to be shrouded in mystery. One interpretation given to landlord Derek Hamilton by "an expert in pub nomenclature" is that it means a beacon or look-out point.

There could be some truth in this because the building commands an extensive perspective across the Rivelin Valley to Stannington. However, it could be that it takes its name from the area immediately to the north which is marked on the Ordnance Survey maps as "Bell Hagg". The explanation may be much simpler. The word "Hagg" means "an area of holly trees" and the Rivelin Valley is extraordinarily rich in these, a feature reflected in the widespread use of the word "Hagg" in local places names. A casual glance at the map reveals Fox Hagg Farm, Fox Hagg and Rough Hagg in the vicinity.

The Bell Hagg

The pub itself dates from 1832 when a certain Dr. Hodgson wished to make a donation to the church at Stannington. Hodgson was a man of dubious moral character, being known throughout Sheffield as a heavy gambler and frequenter of ale houses. Therefore the vicar, having scruples, declined the doctor's offer. Offended by this and in a fit of pique, Hodgson built the Bell Hagg in a prominent position on the opposite side of the valley to the church. The result was that every time the vicar looked through the windows of his vicarage he could not avoid seeing the offending building.

Although it appears normal from its frontage on the A57, it is built on a very steep slope with the result that its rear is more than 80 feet high, a feature which transforms it into a conspicuous landmark when viewed from Stannington and the north. Originally it was named "Hodgson's Choice" but, two years after its construction it became known as "Hodgson's Folly".

During the later years of the nineteenth century the cellars, because they were escape proof, were used to house prisoners and convicts overnight while on their way from the Sheffield Assizes to Strangeways Prison in Manchester. Today the Bell Hagg has a more welcoming atmosphere, its small bar divided into two cosy sections with old-fashioned settles and half-panelled walls which house displays of prints, plates, and copperware.

On offer are Theakston's XB, Stone's Best Bitter, Tetley's Bitter and Boddington's Bitter. These, along with a rotation of guest beers, are all on hand pump. An interesting range of bar meals is available.

Opening Times: Mondays to Saturdays, 11.00 a.m. to 11.00 p.m.; Sundays, 12.00 a.m. to 3.00 p.m. and 7.00 p.m. to 10.30 p.m.

The Rivelin Valley

For centuries the Rivelin Valley was a hive of industrial activity, the river being impounded into numerous small dams many of which remain to be seen. The water from these was fed along goits to drive the water wheels for the cutlery workshops and forges which lined the banks.

While most of these have long since disappeared, the water courses provide a variety of habitats for wildlife ranging from coot and moorhen to dipper, grey wagtail and woodpecker.

For centuries the area was noted for its woodlands, trees from the Rivelin Valley being used to build Sheffield's first hospital as long ago as 1664.

The Route

Leave the Rivelin Valley Post Office by walking along the A57 in the direction of Sheffield. After a few yards, and by a footpath sign, turn left onto a path which skirts to the right of a small dam before passing through a car park to reach Rails Road.

Cross to the facing through stile with both a footpath sign and display panel adjacent. Maintain direction with the River Rivelin on your right but separated from you by an ivy-clad wall.

After approximately 60 yards turn right over a stone packhorse bridge and, at the far end, turn left to continue walking downstream through mixed deciduous woodlands where, in spring, countless songbirds provide a continuous musical background.

Eventually the path climbs above and away from the river to a Y-junction. Fork right into the walled lane leading to the A57. Cross to the footpath sign and proceed up the driveway leading to Blackbrook Farm. Stay to the left of the house before crossing the lawn to a wooden stile in the facing fence. Over that, embark on a long and gradual climb

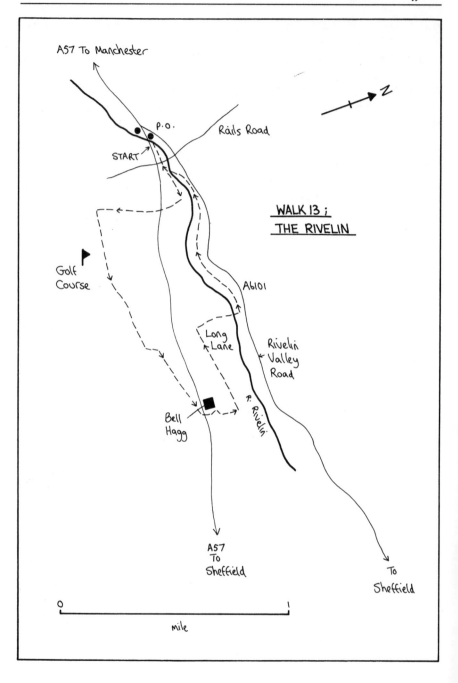

A57 To Manchester

P.O.

Ráils Road

START

N

WALK 13 ;
THE RIVELIN

Golf
Course

A6101

Long
Lane

Rivelin
Valley
Road

P. Rivelin

Bell
Hagg

A57
To
Sheffield

To
Sheffield

0   1

mile

close to the boundary of Blackbrook Wood to a Y-junction by a wall corner and a waymarker post.

Fork left into the woods following an excellent path through the trees as it gains height quickly with Black Brook on your left. At this point, there are no views and hence no artificial excuses for the frequent pauses until you gain a small set of very old stone steps. Dip down to the brook, cross by the stepping stones and resume climbing until meeting a fence of iron railings.

Follow the path round to the left while staying close to the fence and then the wall which eventually replaces it. The path, sometimes very rocky and sometimes very smooth, undulates along the ridge with ever-expanding views in all directions. These embrace Stanage Moors, Stannington, the Loxley Valley, Moscar Heights and the northern and western areas of the city.

In places care is needed because the ground on your left falls dramatically away into the woods. There are patches of heather mixed with gorse and bilberry so providing some idea of the natural vegetation of this upland area where the paths stays consistently above the 1,000 foot contour. Remember that this is well within the Sheffield City boundary!

After a considerable distance an intersection of footpaths is reached. Although unsigned, it is recognisable by a trickle of a stream and an ancient and solitary gatepost by the corner of a housing estate on your right.

Turn left for an extremely steep and rocky descent on a path that is not invariably distinct until, after a distance of about 200 yards, you emerge onto Coppice Lane. Turn right and, ignoring the first public bridleway sign on your left, continue along this broad track as it climbs gradually through the bilberry.

Pass a footpath sign on the right and, 20 yards later, go between two gateposts. Immediately turn left along a path for five yards and, at the junction, maintain direction round the boundary wall of the house on your right. Soon the path becomes stepped as it drops to rendezvous with the A57 opposite the Bell Hagg public house.

Leaving the Bell Hagg, turn left along the A57 for some 40 yards. By the bus stop turn left into the signed footpath for a descent between two stone walls until meeting the rear corner of the Bell Hagg itself.

There make an acute right turn and pass through a disused quarry complete with picnic tables but, after 60 yards, turn left to a five-barred gate after a further 70 yards. Through the gate make a right turn to traverse a sloping field. Leave this by a stone step stile before maintaining direction over the subsequent field to a collapsed stile.

Over this, turn left. Stay to the right of the stone wall while descending the field to another stone step stile. Continue in the same direction across the next field to another stile which provides access onto Long Lane. Turn left through the stile.

Walled on both sides, the lane passes through the valley bottom pastures. Ignore Small Hill Farm with its threatening notices and continue to Windle Hill farm

100 yards beyond this, and by an old stone barn enveloped in ivy, leave the lane by maintaining direction along a field boundary to a telegraph pole which has a waymarker post adjacent.

There turn right aiming for a clump of large trees. By these, veer right across the field corner to a stone step stile. Over that cling to the wall on your left until you cross the River Rivelin by a footbridge to reach a footpath sign. Turn left to walk upstream along the wide, level path.

Notice the succession of weirs and small dams used for creating the goits which sometimes run on your right as small streams. There is also an abundance of dippers with their Persil-white chests bobbing about on the rocks midstream as they hunt for food.

At a Y-junction fork right onto the path which moves towards and runs parallel to Rivelin Valley Road for a short distance before returning to accompany the river back to Rails Road. Pass through the car park as you utilise your outward route for the return to your starting point at the Post Office.

Walk 14. Lodge Moor

A route which traverses moorland, passes alongside reservoirs and uses tracks and field paths for a charming circuit on the western side of Sheffield.

Route: Lodge Moor – The Sportsman – Redmires Conduit – Wyming Brook – Reddicar Clough – Rivelin Dams – Fox Hagg – Lodge Moor

Start: The bus terminus, Redmires Road, Lodge Moor. Map reference 285863.

Distance: 5 miles.

Map: "Sheffield", number 743 in the Ordnance Survey's "Pathfinder" series.

Public Transport: There are frequent bus services to Lodge Moor from Sheffield Interchange (Pond Street) in the city centre.

By Car: The start may be reached by following the road from Tapton Hill through Sandygate and Hallam Road to Lodge Moor Hospital (signed). Alternatively it may be approached from the A57 near Rivelin Bridge, Map reference 291872, by using Lodge Lane and turning right into Redmires Road. There is ample roadside parking but car users may prefer to commence the walk at Wyming Brook car park, further along Redmires Road at map reference 269859.

Refreshments: The Sportsman and the Three Merry Lads, both on Redmires Road, serve bar meals at lunch times and in the evenings.

The Sportsman

This old pub stands on the edge of the moors yet within sight of the city centre. The thick oak beams which still bear the marks of the adze which cut and shaped them form one of the outstanding features of the bar. According to landlord Trevor Snell that was at least 300 years ago, perhaps longer, when the building started life as a farmhouse. It was transformed into a pub when a licence was granted permitting it to serve ale and beer to the Irish navvies who worked on the construction of the Redmires Reservoirs during the early nineteenth century.

The beams are matched by bow windows and the woodwork on the plaster walls which give the impression of magpie architecture. In turn these walls form the background for a display of ancient maps, old black and white photographs of the pub itself and even reproductions of some of Constable's paintings. In no uncertain terms it generates a feeling of warmth, cosiness and hospitality which contrasts the harsh moorland environment outside. The thirsty walker can select from John Smith's Bitter, John Smith's Magnet, Directors' Bitter and Webster's Yorkshire Bitter, all on hand pump. If these fail to tempt there is an equally impressive choice of lagers including Foster's and Carlsberg.

Opening Times: Mondays to Saturdays, 11.30 a.m. to 4.30 p.m. (but variable) and 6.30 p.m. to 11.00 p.m.; Sundays, 12.00 a.m. to 3.00 p.m. and 7.00 p.m. to 10.30 p.m.

The Sportsman

The Rivelin Dams

As with most towns Sheffield originally drew its water supplies from a collection of springs, notably those in Pond Street, now covered by the Sheffield Interchange, and Barker's Pool. When these proved inadequate because of the growth of the population, private water companies constructed small reservoirs. By the early nineteenth century, however, even these failed to assuage the thirst of the citizens and the demands of the growing steel industry so the Corporation assumed responsibility.

During a period of 50 years from 1830 many new reservoirs were built including the two at Rivelin which were completed in 1848. The higher reservoir has a capacity of 48,000,000 gallons while the lower one stores

175,000,000. The water is drawn from a catchment area covering 1,890 acres.

An underground tunnel, completed in 1909, links the Rivelin Reservoirs with those at Derwent, a distance of four and a half miles. It emerges by Wyming Brook Drive at the side of the lower of the two dams.

The Route

From the bus terminus at Lodge Moor, walk along Redmires Road for some 250 yards to the Sportsman pub. By the far corner and a footpath sign, turn left along a footpath flanked by a wall on the right and a shed and the Sportsman on the left. Beyond these, maintain direction across a large football field with a plantation approximately 100 yards away to your right and Lodge Moor Hospital visible to your left.

Aim for the clearly visible path which is directly ahead. On reaching this there is a low wall on your left and, within 80 yards, a waymarker post. By this turn right along the permissive footpath created by Yorkshire Water PLC which follows the line of the Redmires Conduit. If, by this stage you are feeling exhausted, there is a convenient seat on which to rest your weary limbs. On your immediate right is the plantation while, a short distance away to your left is Peat Farm. The entire area consists of upland pasture.

Pass through a wooden barrier designed to deter motor cyclists and find a partially derelict stone wall on your left and a fence on your right where a field has replaced the plantation. Directly ahead are the Peak District Moors but, by now, Wyming Brook Farm is much closer to hand on your right.

Eventually the path develops into a walled lane before passing through another wooden barrier by a footpath sign to emerge onto Brown Hills Lane. Turn right along the road for approximately 100 yards to a T-junction. Turn left along Redmires Road and walk downhill ignoring two footpath signs on your right.

Instead, stay along the road but, after 200 yards from the T-junction, cross Wyming Brook Bridge and then turn right into the car park. Some ten yards beyond the Information Board with its map of the path network, and with Wyming Brook on your right, fork left and climb for some five yards to a Y-junction. Go left, staying just to the right of a stone wall. There is a vast expanse of bracken, bilberry and silver birch to your right.

The path, now on peat, makes for excellent walking with the added

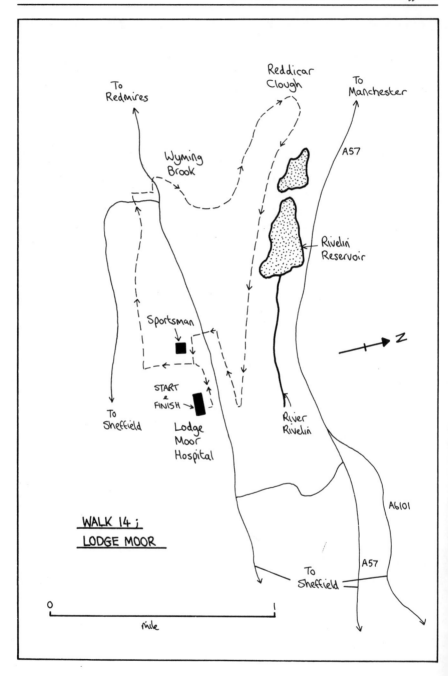

To Redmires

Reddicar Clough

To Manchester

Wyming Brook

A57

Rivelin Reservoir

Sportsman

N

To Sheffield

START & FINISH

River Rivelin

Lodge Moor Hospital

A6101

A57

To Sheffield

WALK 14 ;
LODGE MOOR

0   1
            mile

dimension of moorland expanses in all directions. Soon, even the right-hand side is dominated by heather.

On arriving at a Y-junction by a wall corner on your left, maintain direction to the right of a wall with a distant view of Malin Bridge away in the distance to the east. Where this wall corners to the left continue forward across open moorland while gradually losing height to enter woodland consisting principally of a mixture of oak and coniferous trees.

Here, the path levels to stay with the contour but, by the woodland boundary, drops steeply to a waymarker post. From this it continues the steep descent to a plank footbridge. From the far end, stay forwards for 100 yards to meet Wyming Brook Drive at the foot of Reddicar Clough. Turn right along the broad bridleway.

There is a brook on the left as you progress through mixed woodlands. The going is level and progress swift. On reaching a Y-junction by an old-fashioned footpath signpost, fork left downhill.

Beyond a somewhat large U-bend the first of the Rivelin Reservoirs appears on the left presenting a scene of peace and tranquillity against a backdrop of trees with the tips of the moors rising behind. By the entrance gate to Fox Holes Lodge, turn right over a stone step stile with a footpath sign alongside and walk a level path through the trees for 200 yards to a Y-junction.

Fork right for a steepish climb through more trees until meeting a much wider path running along the contour. Turn left along this and cross a plank footbridge. About 15 yards beyond swing right, following the main path uphill. If you are fortunate in the time of year, you may be accompanied by the call of the cuckoo. Finally, leave the woods for a more open aspect dominated by scattered patches of heather and bilberry.

Pass to the left of two gateposts and, shortly afterwards, pass a solitary one. From this the path resumes its climb until reaching a waymarker post. Make an acute turn to the right, more or less retracing your steps but now much higher. The Rivelin Reservoirs are in view again but now well down below and to your right.

After a further short climb the path levels to cling to the contour with a wall and fence on your left and there are numerous clumps of foxglove.

At the next waymarker post, situated by a wall corner, turn left along a clear path which crosses a small field to Redmires Road by the Three Merry Lads pub. Turn left along the road to reach the Sportsman and then, subsequently, your starting point.

Walk 15. Porter Brook

Starting almost in the heart of Sheffield, this route follows the
course of Porter Brook, passing Shepherd Wheel and Forge
Dam before climbing to the tiny moorland hamlet of
Ringinglow which is within the city boundary and yet on the
very edge of the National Park.

Route: Bingham Park – Shepherd Wheel – Forge Dam – Carr Bridge –
Porter Clough – Ringinglow

Start: The junction of Rustlings Road and Oakbrook Road. Map reference
321859.

Finish: The Norfolk Arms, Ringinglow. Map reference 291837

Distance: 3½ miles.

Map: "Sheffield", number 743 in the Ordnance Survey's "Pathfinder" series.

Public Transport: The start is served by bus number 86 from Pinstone
Street to Fulwood.   Ringinglow has frequent daily buses from Sheffield
except for Sundays in the winter.

By Car: Leave the city centre along Eccleshall Road (A625) to Hunter's Bar
and then turn right along Rustlings Road. Parking is restricted to side streets.
For Ringinglow, leave Sheffield by the A625 and then take Ringinglow Road
from Eccleshall. From the west leave the A625 along a minor road a short
distance east of the Fox House Inn. Ample off-road parking opposite the
Norfolk Arms.

Refreshments: There is a cafe serving light refreshments and beverages at
Forge Dam. The Norfolk Arms also serves bar meals at lunch times and in
the evenings.

Museums: Shepherd's Wheel – Opening Times: Wednesday to Saturdays 10.00 a.m. to 12.30 p.m. and 1.30 p.m. to 5.00 p.m.; Sundays: 11.00
a.m. to 12.30 p.m. and 1.30 p.m. to 5.00 p.m. (4.00 p.m. in winter); Closed
on Monday and Tuesday throughout the year. Telephone – Sheffield (0742)
367731.

The Norfolk Arms

Built of grey stone, and rectangular in shape with castellations, The
Norfolk Arms is possessed of a rather gaunt exterior which matches
exactly its position on the moorland fringes west of Sheffield.

The Norfolk Arms

Inside, however, there is a warm welcome from landlord Timothy Robert Noakes. The bar, with its wooden beams, wainscotted walls and carpeted floors is extremely cosy. Hunting and other types of horn are abundant and so are the countryside scenes. When the weather is cold a roaring log fire blazes away. Surprisingly the Oak Lounge is large with tables and chairs arranged around a small dance floor. The fireplace has a large canopy supported by wooden pillars and bears the Norfolk coat-of-arms. The walls are decorated with a selection of pistols and other firearms, and horse harness plus more paintings of rural scenes.

Cask conditioned Stone's Best Bitter, Bass and Worthington's Best Bitter are on sale in addition to the usual selection of lagers and wines. The bar also sports a fine array of malt whiskies. A large menu of bar meals is available all day.

Opening Times: Mondays to Saturdays, 11.00 a.m. to 11.00 p.m.; Sundays, 12.00 a.m. to 3.00 p.m. and 7.00 p.m. to 10.30 p.m.

The Route

Alighting from the number 84 bus at the junction of Rustlings Road with Oakbrook Road, turn left through the entrance into Bingham Park which was donated to the City of Sheffield by Sir James Bingham in 1911.

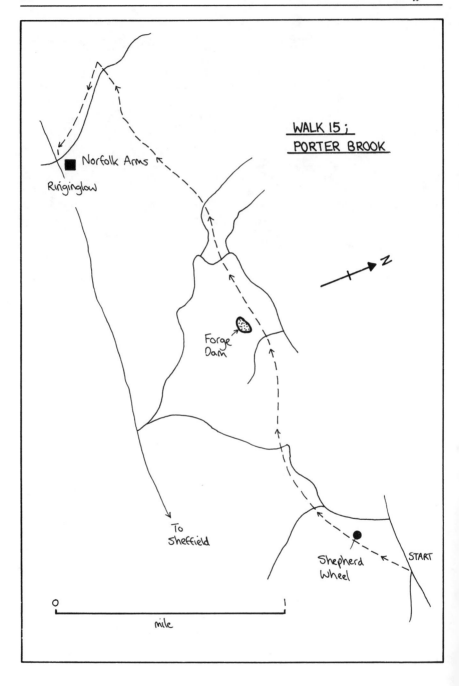

WALK 15 ;
PORTER BROOK

Norfolk Arms

Ringinglow

Forge
Dam

To
Sheffield

Shepherd
Wheel

START

0   1

mile

Follow the main surfaced drive, with a defined cycle track on the left-hand side. Initially the Porter Brook is not evident but the steep slopes on the left are clothed with a rich mixture of broad-leaved trees.

By Hanging Water, a small cascade, the Porter makes its appearance on the right. Continue along the driveway for approximately half a mile until reaching another of Sheffield's numerous small museums devoted to its peculiar industrial heritage. This is Shepherd Wheel, a water-powered grinding works believed to have been used for the grinding of table and other domestic knives, including pen knives. An inspection of the interior will provide ample evidence of the horrendous working conditions endured by the men employed there. Originally known as the Porter Wheel, it was mentioned in the will of a cutler during the reign of Queen Elizabeth I. In the following century there are frequent references to it in the rent books of the Earls of Shrewsbury. It acquired its present name from a certain Mr. Shepherd who employed about a dozen men there in the late eighteenth century. As with so many of these small enterprises Shepherd's Wheel ceased production during the 1930s. Restoration work was undertaken by the City Council in 1968 with the dredging of the mill race followed by renovations of the over-shot water wheel which is still turning.

Leaving the museum maintain direction until the path meets Highcliffe Road on a sharp U-bend. Porter Bridge is on the left. Cross directly and, within 40 yards, cross a small bridge so that Porter Brook in on your left as you walk through Whitely Woods. After some 500 yards a small flight of stone steps leads up to Whitely Wood Road. Make a left turn over the bridge and, at the far end, turn right by the footpath sign.

Within 20 yards a Y-junction is reached. Fork left so that the Porter is now on your right as the path loses its surface. Hereabouts in springtime the woods are carpeted with anemones, wild garlic and celandines while overhead is a large rookery which comes as something of a surprise being so close to the city centre.

Soon a stone memorial is seen through the trees on your left. A short diversion up the steep path leads to the classical style monument erected in 1922 to the memory of Thomas Bolsolver. The inventor of Sheffield Plate, he lived in the nearby Whitely Wood Hall from 1762 to 1788. Retracing your steps re-join the main route. At the next junction turn right along the surfaced path to meet Ivy Cottage Lane within 20 yards.

Turn left along the road for 20 yards and then turn right by a footpath sign to pass a children's playground on your right before reaching Forge Dam Cafe which takes its name from the forge which once occupied the site. Continue beyond the cafe to reach the dam where mallard, coot and moorhen are always to be seen. Walk to the right until reaching the diametrically opposed corner of the dam, Cross the stone footbridge to a Y-junction. Fork right to pass to the left of two small weirs on the Porter Brook.

The path becomes wider and the aspect more rural with a tree-lined ridge ahead. After passing through a metal barrier Carr Bridge is reached. Cross to the footpath signed Porter Brook and, at another Y-junction within 100 yards, fork right to a footbridge. Negotiate a through stile with a footpath sign adjacent and cross another road to enter Clough Lane which is signed as a bridleway.

This runs between stone walls with hills on either side. Ignore the first footpath sign on the left, staying forward along the lane which swings right over a stone bridge. At the far end of this turn left by a footpath sign to begin the long, steep climb through the thickly wooded Porter Clough with the brook now little more than an upland stream.

In the higher reaches of the clough cross two small footbridges in quick succession before arriving at a footpath sign. By this turn left in the direction of Ringinglow, soon crossing a small footbridge and climbing even further before making an exit onto Fulwood Lane by a small car park.

Turn left along the road for a quarter of a mile to the junction of Fulwood Lane with Ringinglow Road in the centre of the hamlet of Ringinglow. Turn left for the final few yards to the Norfolk Arms.

Toll House, Ringinglow

Walk 16. Abbeydale

Commencing on the high moorlands to the west of the city, this linear route descends through mixed woodlands to the residential suburb of Abbeydale.

Route: Ringinglow – Limb Valley – Whirlow Bridge – Ryecroft Glen – Abbeydale

Start: The junction of Ringinglow Road and Sheephill Road, opposite the Norfolk Arms, Ringinglow. Map reference 291837.

Finish: Dore Junction railway station, Abbeydale. Map reference 324813.

Distance: 3½ miles.

Map: "Sheffield", number 743 in the Ordnance Survey's "Pathfinder" series.

Public Transport: Ringinglow has frequent daily buses from Sheffield. (not winter Sundays). Buses from Chesterfield on summer Sundays and Bank Holidays. Dore Junction has daily train services from Sheffield and Manchester. Several bus routes to the city centre.

Refreshments: The Norfolk Arms, Ringinglow. Open Mondays to Saturdays 11.00 a.m. to 11.00 p.m. Sundays 12.00 a.m. to 3.00 p.m. and 7.00 to 10.30 p.m. Bar meals served all day. The Dore Junction (see below). The Abbeydale Industrial Hamlet serves light meals and refreshments between April and October.

Museums:: The Abbeydale Industrial Hamlet – situated on Abbeydale Road South near the end of the walk. Opening hours: Tuesdays to Saturdays, all year, 10.00 a.m. to 5.00 p.m. Sundays, 11.00 a.m. to 5.00 p.m. Closed Mondays.

The Dore Junction

Converted from the former railway station this must be one of the few pubs in Britain with regular service trains stopping by the door. As you enter there is a tiny bar with a larger lounge to your right. This has the original tongue and groove ceiling timbers and beams, now painted white. The entire room is filled with railway memorabilia including a large station clock, engine nameplates, signs and posters, especially from the days of steam. There are railway maps which pre-date Beeching's axe.

The Dore Junction

On offer are Theakston's Old Peculier, Timothy Taylor's Bitter, Burglar Bill's Double Bagger and Old Mill from the Snaith Brewery. In addition there is a constantly changing choice of guest beers. Bar meals are available and there is also a small restaurant.

Opening Times: Mondays: closed lunch time. 5.30 p.m. to 11.00 p.m.; Tuesday to Saturday, 12.00 a.m. to 3.00 p.m. and 5.30 p.m. to 11.00 p.m.; Sundays, 12.00 a.m. to 3.00 p.m. and 7.00 to 10.30 p.m.

Abbeydale Industrial Hamlet

This is a major industrial complex dating back to the eighteenth century and resembles many others which used to be in existence throughout Sheffield.

It includes a water-driven tilt forge and grinding shop plus a Huntsman Crucible Furnace. There are workers' cottages, a manager's house furnished in the style of Victorian Sheffield, offices, and warehouses. Until this century, the hamlet specialised in the production of steel scythe blades which were exported world wide.

The Route

From the road junction in Ringinglow pass to the left of the Cupola Toll House and walk along Sheephill Road. After 100 yards, and just be the end of the last house, turn left over a stone step stile with a footpath sign adjacent.

With Limb Brook on your left, descend the large field with its open views while aiming for a prominent patch of reeds. Negotiate these by using the flagged path to reach the first junction.

Ignore a path to the right, instead staying forward along more flags to a footpath sign. At this point there is a derelict stone building on your right. By the sign, fork left for 50 yards to a second footpath sign. By this turn right through a squeezer stile, descend a short flight of steps and, at the bottom, turn left to enter woodlands.

As the path loses height it crosses and re-crosses the brook by a series of small footbridges with the valley flanks getting steeper all the time. These are covered with mature, mixed broad-leaved trees while the City Council has provided benches and picnic sites at intervals. Eventually, the path widens and climbs to embark on an undulating course through Bole Hill Plantation with the Limb Brook down below on the right.

On gaining a T-junction with a footpath sign minus one arm and a path going off to the right, maintain direction down the valley to a second signed junction. Again stay forward to pass to the left of Whirlow Brook Park. If you pass this way in April look for the American Skunk Cabbages with their brilliant yellow spathes.

By the far corner of the park the track meets a lay-by on Eccleshall Road South at the very point where it becomes Hathersage Road. Turn right for a few yards to the main road. Turn right again, pass the Park entrance and continue for 50 yards. Turn left, cross Eccleshall Road South into Limb Lane and, almost immediately and by a footpath sign, turn left into Ryecroft Glen. There is a hedge on your right beyond which is a large playing field complete with soccer and rugby pitches. There is also a good view of the western areas of Sheffield.

50 yards beyond where the hedge terminates, and by a derelict building which is the site of the former Whirlow Wheel (another reminder of Sheffield's industrial past), the wide track ends.

Turn right and, keeping a line of coniferous trees on your immediate left, walk along the edge of the playing field. Leave through a squeezer stile set into the facing stone wall some 20 yards to the right of the field corner. Swing right to a Y-junction after 10 yards. Fork right. The steep land on your left is a bird sanctuary which, according to the latest survey

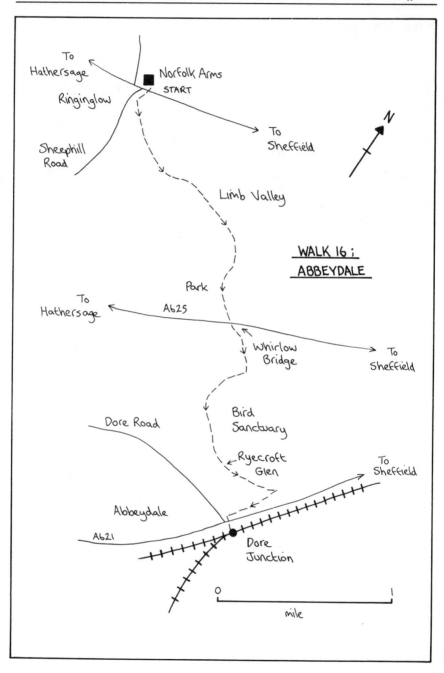

work carried out by the Sorby Natural History Society, has 61 species of birds, a mixture of resident breeders and summer migrants.

The path arcs through this western area of Eccleshall Woods which were given to Sheffield by the Earl Fitzwilliam and opened by Princess Mary in 1928. They are a mixture of oak, birch, elm and holly with an under storey of bramble. In spring the floor is carpeted with flowers. Until comparatively recent times the timber from these woodlands was used for the manufacture of charcoal employed in the manufacture of steel.

At the next T-junction turn left along the Abbeydale to Dore bridle-way. On reaching the next junction, turn left following the path signed to Abbeydale. Within 100 yards cross a concrete footbridge and, at the far end, turn right. The track, lined with stone kerbs after the fashion of an early tramway, corkscrews its way through the woodlands before reaching the A621, Abbeydale Road South.

Turn right for the final 400 yards to the Dore Junction which is on your left. Alternatively, a left turn will lead directly to the Abbeydale Industrial Hamlet after approximately the same distance.

Walk 17. Owler Bar

A circular route using well-trodden paths and bridleways
which embraces an outward journey through silent
woodlands with a return across wild, sweeping moorland just
beyond the city limits.

Route: Owler Bar — Greave's Piece — Foxland Plantation — Bole Hill —
Ramsley Reservoir — Big Moor — Barbrook Reservoir — Saltersitch Bridge —
Owler Bar

Start: Owler Bar. Map reference 294780

Distance: 7¼ miles.

Map: "The Peak District: White Peak Area", number 24 in the Ordnance
Survey's "Outdoor Leisure" series.

Public Transport: Owler bar is served by daily buses (including Sundays)
from Sheffield, Bakewell, Buxton, Baslow and Hanley. On summer Sundays
and Bank Holidays there are services from Chesterfield and Crystal Peaks.

By Car: Owler Bar is at the junction of the A621 Sheffield to Baslow road
with the B6054, the Fox House to Dronfield road and the B6051 to Chesterfield. There is no official car park but several places in the vicinity provide for
off-road parking.

Refreshments: The Peacock Hotel (see below).

The Peacock

Set back from the complicated road junction at Owler Bar, just beyond
the city boundary, this well known landmark is a sturdy building of
local Derbyshire millstone grit.

Dating from the very early years of the seventeenth century, the road
originally ran behind it but in 1802 the Duke of Devonshire, who owned
it, had it rebuilt in its present position facing the road. Situated at such
a vital junction, it is hardly surprising that it became a famous posting
inn during the stage coach era and, as a reminder of those days, the Toll
Bar Cottage still stands alongside.

Inside, it still retains something of the Dickensian ambience of this
period, especially in the public bar with its original oak-beamed ceiling
and cream coloured walls divided magpie style with more woodwork.

The Peacock

There is an abundance of copper and brassware, the one concession to modernism being the plush upholstered banquettes lining the walls. Landlord Antonio Ferandes serves Stone's Best Bitter and Worthington's Bitter as well as lagers, wines and spirits. In addition to the formal restaurant, bar meals are served at lunch time and in the evening.

Opening Times: Mondays to Saturdays, 11.30 a.m. to 3.00 p.m. and 5.30 p.m. to 11.00 p.m.; Sundays, 12.00 a.m. to 3.00 p.m. and 7.00 p.m. to 10.30 p.m.

The Route

Leaving the Peacock turn right for a short distance before forking left into the A621 Bakewell road. Even at this early stage there is a fantastic view of Sheffield, North Derbyshire and the White Peak. The landscape has a well-wooded appearance, a reminder that the word "Owler" in "Owler Bar" is derived from the Alder tree.

Pass a milestone on the left, indicating a distance of nine miles from Sheffield, and 100 yards further on, opposite a white gate, turn left through an unsigned gateway onto a grass track descending through

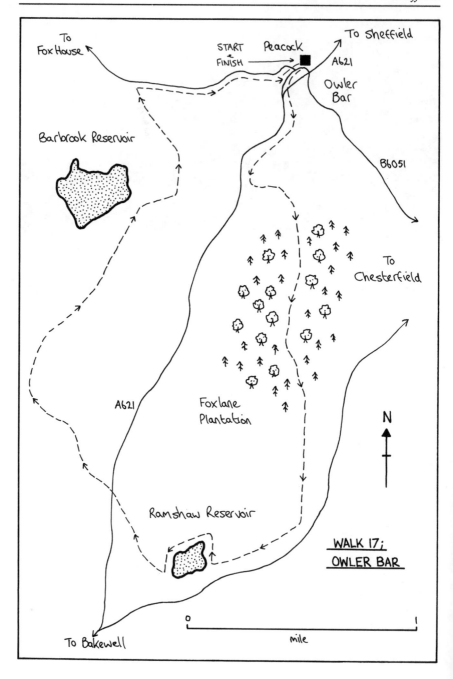

To Fox House

To Sheffield

START
FINISH

Peacock

A621

Owler
Bar

Barbrook Reservoir

B6051

To
Chesterfield

A621

Foxlane
Plantation

N

Ramshaw Reservoir

WALK 17;
OWLER BAR

To Bakewell

0   1
                    mile

bracken and a bank of bilberry with Greave's Piece on your right. In spring there are bluebells and the song of the skylark. As the paths drops lower into the valley, more scrub appears.

After passing between two isolated gateposts cross a rough track and stay forward into Foxland Plantation. Initially there is a gentle ascent on a wide path through a mixture of birch and rowan with Hewett's Bank occasionally glimpsed through the trees on your left.

Soon the going levels. After a further mile emerge from the woodland to be greeted by four rusty upturned baths on your right and a small pond where mallard often swim. On the crest of Hewett's Bank there are several hawthorns sculpted by decades of wind into weird, artistic shapes.

At the next junction, with a path coming in from your left, stay forward to reach the road junction at Bole Hill. Turn right along Fox Lane, the road signed to Baslow. In the far distance ahead but slightly to the left are views of Gardoms Edge and Birchen Edge. Beyond them another visible landmark is Stanton Moor.

After half a mile turn right through a white gate to follow the very green grassy path to the right of Ramsley Reservoir which is cupped by heather moorland. By the far corner of the reservoir swing left over a small stone bridge to follow the path to the next corner where there is a footpath finger post.

Turn left again. A wildlife sanctuary on your right is home to golden plover, meadow pipit and skylark.

A T-junction is reached by the third corner of the reservoir, recognised by a metal bridge over an exit outflow and a five-barred gate on your left. Turn right, as indicated by a waymark. The excellent grass path winds its way through bilberry and heather with a prospect of Big Moor and White Edge in the middle distance.

After half a mile a stone step stile adjacent to a white five-barred gate provides access to the A621. Cross diagonally right to a stone step stile alongside another white five-barred gate. Another excellent wide grass path winds its way along the contour over Big Moor and alongside Bar Brook, eventually meeting a small lake which has been fenced-off by National Park Rangers. It has been provided with duck islands to encourage the return of wildfowl. On my visit Canada Geese were nesting.

Beyond this lake the path rises steadily with Big Moor. Cross a stone footbridge and then continue climbing until crossing a small concrete bridge with metal railings. Although not visible at this point Barbrook Reservoir is but a short distance to the left, shielded by a small ridge.

Maintain direction towards an isolated stone house. With this about

100 yards to your left there is a footpath finger at a T-junction. Turn right along the concessionary path which is surfaced because it is the approach road to the reservoir. After 300 yards and at an intersection of paths, with another finger post adjacent, turn left onto another very green path which traverses the moors for approximately a quarter of a mile to another junction.

Veer towards the left while maintaining your general direction. Barbrook Reservoir is now clearly visible to your left.

After half a mile you reach a small wooden gate which provides access to the B6054. Turn right to cross Saltersitch Bridge on your way back to the Peacock and Owler Bar.

Walk 18. Totley

A short circular walk on the very outskirts of the city embracing some fine moorland prospects followed by an enchanting passage through mixed deciduous woodlands.

Route: Totley – Old Hay – Bents Farms – Penny Lane – Hollin Hill – Totley Brook – New Totley – Totley.

Start: The junction of Hillfoot Road with the A621 in Totley. Map reference 306798.

Distance: 3¼ miles.

Maps: 1. "Sheffield", number 743 in the Ordnance Survey's "Pathfinder" series. "The Peak District, White Peak Area", number 24 in the Ordnance Survey's "Outdoor Leisure" series.

Public Transport: The start is served by frequent daily buses from the city centre and several daily buses from Bakewell, Baslow, Buxton and Hanley.

By Car: Totley is on the A621 Sheffield to Baslow road. There is no car park but some limited parking in side roads.

Refreshments: Bar meals are available at the Crown on Hillfoot Road.

The Crown

This old pub, situated on Hillfoot Road not far from the start, was the meeting place for the Barlow Hunt until as recently as 1936 and, to emphasise the point, there are several sepia photographs hanging on the walls of the bar. Typically there is a low ceiling with some old, thick wooden beams which help to emphasise the antiquity of the building. This genuine authentic atmosphere is reinforced by several areas of exposed stonework and thick walls.

The carpeted bar is large but subdivided into smaller sections to increase the snug, friendly atmosphere created by landlord John Robert Abbott. His bar meals are excellent with a strong but far from exclusive emphasis on fish dishes. These can be washed down with Stone's Best Bitter or a selection of lagers.

Opening Times: Monday to Saturday, 11.30 a.m. to 3.00 p.m. and 5.30 p.m. to 11.00 p.m. Sundays, 12.00 a.m. to 3.00 p.m. and 7.00 p.m. to 10.30 p.m.

The Crown

Totley Bents

The area known as Totley Bents derives it name from bent grass, a tough species with broad leaves which is found on moorland. It is sometimes referred to as Benty Grass and for some reason cattle refuse to eat it. In the Sheffield area, especially on the moorland edges, Bent is occasionally to be found in a field name.

The Route

Leaving the A621 turn down Hillfoot Road, soon passing a small school on your left. At the bottom of the hill by the junction with Penny Lane stands the Crown. Suitably refreshed, continue along Hillfoot Road for a further 250 yards before turning left by a footpath sign and passing through a gateway onto a track.

Pass the house, Old Hay, on your right before coming face-to-face with a substantial stone house. Stay to the left of this, climb a short flight of steps to a stone step stile behind the house and cross the ensuing field by staying close to the wall on your right.

Follow this round the field corner and turn right over a stone step stile adjacent to a five-barred gate. Advance towards Bents farm. By the

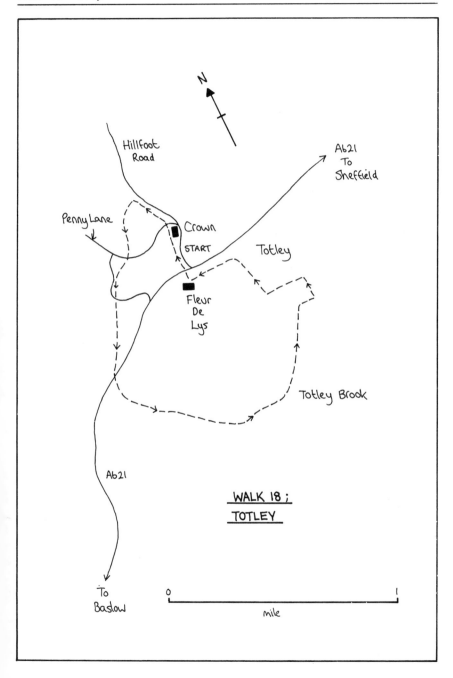

N

Hillfoot
Road

Ab21
To
Sheffield

Penny Lane

Crown

START

Totley

Fleur
De
Lys

Totley Brook

Ab21

WALK 18 ;
TOTLEY

To
Baslow

0   1

mile

buildings negotiate a wooden stile before turning left through a five-barred gate to reach Penny Lane.

Turn right but, after 10 yards, go left into Lane Head Road. A very short distance beyond Monny Brook Cattery follow the road round to the left but, at the bottom of the dip and by a footpath sign, turn right into a lane. After 30 yards take the flagged path to the right of the ford, cross a tiny footbridge and turn left over a stile onto a planked footbridge.

Faced by a red sign warning of a rifle range, turn right by a waymarker post to work your way through the gorse before the path veers to the left up the slope to meet the A621.

Turn right for some splendid views over Totley Moor towards Owler Bar. After 100 yards, leave the main road by turning left over a step stile. Taking your direction from the arm of the footpath sign, veer right across the corner of the field to another stone step stile within 100 yards. Over that turn left to meet a Y-junction immediately. Fork right along the clear path as indicated by the waymark. Ignoring an obvious ladder stile on your right, stay forward with a conifer plantation on your left.

Soon a wooden stile provides access to Gillfield Wood which consists of mixed deciduous species. This is arguably the most attractive woodland within the city limits. In early summer it boasts an extensive covering of bluebells and resounds to the call of the cuckoo.

After some distance Totley Brook flows in from your right to accompany you on your walk. For many centuries this tiny stream has formed the boundary between Yorkshire and Derbyshire.

Continue along the well-maintained footpath for a considerable distance until reaching a Y-junction. Fork right for 10 yards to an intersection of paths. Maintain your direction, downstream. Within 100 yards pass between two gateposts with another pair within a very short distance.

After well over a mile a wooden stile followed by a footbridge provides an exit from the woods. Maintain direction along a field lying in a very shallow valley with a scattering of hawthorn. Over the next stile continue through more scrub before the path twists to the right to return to the bank of Totley Brook.

Soon houses start to close in but, 100 yards before a scout hut, turn left over a wooden stile and pass between the houses to a footpath sign. Make a right turn into Aldam Road. At the next junction go left into Green Oak Road. Where this meets Main Avenue turn right and continue until reaching the A621. Turn left for the short distance to the starting point.

Walk 19. Graves Park

A linear route starting out through Graves Park and passing Norton Church before descending steeply to the inner city at Heeley.

Route: Meadowhead — Graves Park — Hemsworth Road — Backmoor — Hemsworth — Heeley.

Start: The junction of Meadowhead with Charles Ashmore Road. Map reference 349819

Finish: Richards Road, Heeley. Map reference 358848.

Distance: 3½ miles.

Maps: 1. "Sheffield", number 743 in the Ordnance Survey's "Pathfinder" series. 2. "A to Z" Sheffield Street Atlas.

Public Transport: Both start and finish are served by frequent buses from the city centre, services 434 and 439.

By Car: For Graves Park follow the A61 Chesterfield road from the city centre. Car parks in the park. For the finish in Richards Road follow the B6388 from the city centre. No parking in Richards Road but ample space in Cat Lane nearby.

Refreshments: The kiosk on Graves Park serves beverages and snacks. The cafe in Graves Park is open on Thursdays and Fridays from 10.30 a.m. to 3.30 p.m. and on Saturdays and Sundays from 10.30 p.m. to 4.00 p.m. The New Inn, Hemsworth Road, serves bar meals at lunch times and in the evenings.

The New Inn

A new-ish red-brick building on Hemsworth Road, the New Inn is one of Tetley's Big Steak Pubs. Not surprisingly it specialises in steak but also offers a wide range of other bar meals from fish dishes to vegetarian. Modernised in 1987, it has a large bar subdivided into cubicles and with one section raised. The pillars are lined with mirrors and the banquettes lining the walls are of plush. The shelves sport a display of copperware and the walls are decorated with some very attractive country scenes and floral pictures. Cyril and Mavis Parisson serve hand-drawn Tetley's Bitter and Marston's Pedigree in addition to a range of wines, lagers and spirits. **Opening Times:** Mondays to Saturdays, 11.30 a.m. to 11.00 p.m.; Sundays, 12.00 a.m. to 3.00 p.m. and 7.00 p.m. to 10.30 p.m.

The New Inn

Norton

Graves is the largest public park in Sheffield, covering 83 hectares. Acquired by the Corporation in three separate stages, 1925, 1932 and 1935, it was previously the estate of Norton Hall.

The parish church of St. James, Norton, has occupied the same site since 1180, possibly replacing an earlier one . There is the stump of a medieval cross in the churchyard. The tower arch and the tower both reflect the Transitional Norman period of architecture as do the rounded pillars on the north side of the transept and the octagonal pillars on the south.

The font dates from 1220. The Blythe Chantry Chapel belongs to a later date, having been added in 1524 by Geoffrey Blythe, Bishop of Lichfield and Coventry in memory of his parents.

On the green outside the churchyard is a tall, thin column, reminiscent of Cleopatra's Needle, bearing the name "Chantry". It stands in memory of Sir Francis Leggat Chantry, who was born near Norton on the 7th April, 1781. Of humble parentage, he was apprenticed to Robert Ramsey, a carver and print seller in Sheffield in 1797 but five years later moved to London.

He acquired a national reputation as the result of numerous busts he executed of famous people, becoming a member of the Royal Academy in 1818. In 1835 he was knighted but died in 1841. He is buried in Norton churchyard. The memorial, erected in 1854, is of Cheeswring granite transported from Cornwall to Hull by sea and then overland to Sheffield. Almost 22 feet high, it is one piece mounted on steps.

The Route

Alighting from the bus at the junction of Meadowhead with Charles Ashmore Avenue, enter Graves Park through the main gates. Immediately inside make a right turn, walking parallel with Charles Ashmore Avenue which is just beyond the park boundary on your right.

On your left are bowling greens, refreshment kiosk and tennis courts. On reaching a junction which has another park entrance to your right and a car park on your left, fork to the right, the path leading over a vast expanse of open parkland which is dotted with trees and coverts of rhododendrons.

At the next cross-roads in the path system stay forward along an unpaved path which quickly acquires metal railed fencing on either side. Normally Highland Cattle are to be seen grazing in the field to your right. By the far corner of this field maintain direction following a path signed to Norton Church, with the imposing classical style Norton Hall on your left.

Exit the park through a narrow gap and turn left along Norton Church Road to the parish church. From the church retrace your steps back into the park and, at the intersection by the far corner of Norton Hall, turn right. Walk between a holly hedge on your right and more metal railings on your left. The path widens, curves round to the left and loses height before passing between two lakes where mallard and coot may be seen.

Continue in the same direction but now climbing towards a black and white building which is the Graves Park Centre and cafe. By this turn right to stay to the left of the animal park with its rare breeds of horses, sheep, pigs and goats before finally leaving Graves Park by the junction of Bunting Nook and Hemsworth Road. Turn right, soon passing John Eaton's Almshouses on your right and Lees Hall Golf Club on your left. By the New Inn turn left into Ashbury Lane which, after 100 yards and by Backmoor, develops into an unadopted road and, subsequently, into a lane.

Pass to the left of a metal gate by some old stone farm buildings and a footpath sign. The track becomes a narrow path to the right of the golf course. From here there is a very good view over the city which is some distance below.

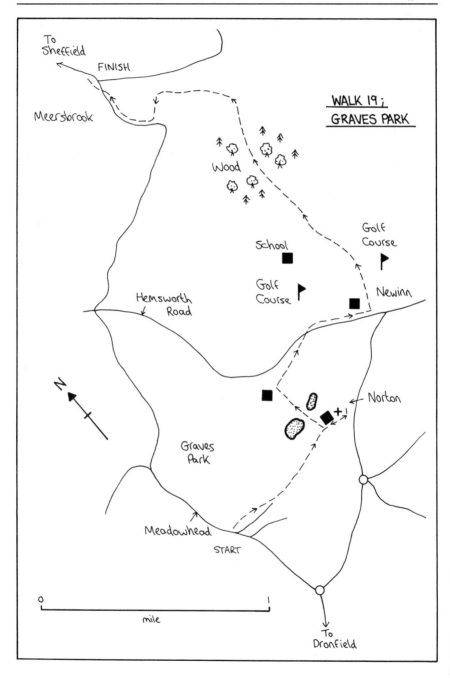

To
Sheffield
FINISH

Meersbrook

WALK 19;
GRAVES PARK

Wood

School

Golf
Course

Golf
Course

Newinn

Hemsworth
Road

N

Norton

Graves
Park

Meadowhead

START

0   1
                mile

To
Dronfield

Staying to the right of an overgrown hedge, the path descends steeply to a couple of steps beyond which the golf course is on both sides. Soon it acquires a cinder surface. At a cross roads in the path network maintain direction but now with Newfield School for Girls on your left. By the far end of the school buildings the path bends round to the right and becomes lined with hawthorn, gorse and bramble.

After a through metal stile enter Coneygree Wood with its mixture of broad-leaved trees. At the next intersection continue in the same direction but with a wider path which continues downhill to yet another junction. Turn left and, after approximately 150 yards, pass through a gateless gateway with a large expanse of allotments appearing well down below on your left.

Go through a metal barrier with a footpath sign and swing to the left. Negotiate a wooden through stile to cross a footbridge with iron railings on the left and a low stone parapet on the right. 30 yards beyond stands Rose Cottage which has been occupied since 1835, a period when this area would have been far more rural.

From this point the path widens into a lane, crosses a second footbridge and reaches a T-junction. Turn left to walk through Carr Woodlands. By a flight of steps on your right, ignore a lane leading off to the left opting, instead, to maintain direction until emerging onto Cat Lane.

Stay along this suburban road with its semi-detached houses as it develops into Northcote Lane. On meeting Albert Road turn right and then left into Carrfield Road. At the far end negotiate the busy traffic island into Richards Road for the bus stop.

Walk 20. Shire Brook

A route combining a surprising mixture of semi-rural scenery
with industrial archaeology.

Route: Golden Plover – Birley Spa – Mosborough Parkway – Penny Loaf –
Rainbow Forge – Stone Lane – Coisley Hill – Dyke Vale Road – Golden
Plover.

Start: The Golden Plover at the junction of Birley Spa Lane with Spa View
Road. Map reference 407835.

Distance: 3 miles.

Map: "Aughton and Carlton in Lindrick", number 744 in the Ordnance
Survey's "Pathfinder" series.

Public Transport: Bus number 41 from Sheffield Interchange (Pond Street)
to the Golden Plover. Frequent daily service.

By Car: Leave Mosborough Parkway at Coisley Hill roundabout and enter
Dyke Vale Road. At the far end turn right into Birley Spa Lane. Roadside
parking.

Refreshments: None on the route.

The Golden Plover

This modern pub has an air of luxury in its large, open bar with
upholstered settles, chairs and carpeted floor. The decor is subdued,
being a mixture of mahogany panelling and soft-toned wallpapers. A
variety of prints are displayed on the walls: some of stately homes, some
of horses and others of country scenes. Landlord Rodney Tyson serves
Bass Special Bitter and Stone's Best Bitter in addition to lagers. There
is a games room and satellite television. No food is served.

    Opening Times: Mondays to Saturdays 11.00 a.m. to 11.00 p.m.;
Sundays 12.00 a.m. to 3.00 p.m. and 7.00 p.m. to 10.30 p.m.

Birley Spa

There is a common belief that the natural spring which supplies water
to Birley Spa was in use during Roman times but there is no written
evidence to suggest the existence of a spa until the early eighteenth
century. Perhaps hoping to emulate the success of Bath and of the Duke

of Devonshire in developing Buxton, Earl Manvers opened Birley Spa as a commercial venture in 1843. The grounds surrounding the spring were laid out as pleasure gardens.

Initially it was a popular venue with people from the surrounding areas but, within 30 years the hotel had closed its doors and only one bath continued in use. This still remains on the lower floor of the Spa building which is not open to the general public today. Before the Second World War the Spa was a popular place for picnics and there was boating on the pond.

The Golden Plover

The Shire Brook

From its size it is almost impossible to imagine but the Shire Brook has almost always formed an important boundary. In early Saxon times it formed the frontier between the kingdoms of Northumbria and Mercia. It was also the dividing line between the jurisdictions of the Archbishop of Canterbury and the Archbishop of York. More locally, until 1974, it was the county boundary between Yorkshire and Derbyshire, hence its name. Today its lies entirely with the City of Sheffield.

From before the Tudor period it was a centre of sickle and scythe manufacture with no fewer than five water wheels operating by 1819.

Associated with these were numerous forges and metal grinding work-shops, notably Carr Forge and Upper and Lower Sickle. Traces of the various dams, their retaining walls and goits may still be seen.

The area between Birley Spa and the Shire Brook, originally a part of Birley Moor, is known as "The Gosh". Until the advent of the deep mine, its numerous bell pits extracted coal for use in the local workshops.

The Route

Leaving the Golden Plover turn right along Birley Spa Lane for 100 yards before forking left down a surfaced lane signed to Birley Spa. Above and to the left is Birley Spa Infant School. After approximately 150 yards the cream coloured spa building is reached. Pass to the left of this but, after a further 50 yards and by a modern house, fork right along a narrow path which descends steeply to the bottom of the slope where a through stile provides access onto Vale Dyke Road.

Cross and turn left for 10 yards before turning right to take the obvious path which runs diagonally to the left with an electricity sub-station on your right. Aim for a gap in the facing hawthorns before passing through the tunnel beneath the Mosborough Parkway.

At the far end turn right for a slight gentle climb with the busy highway to your right and Carr Forge Dam, complete with mallard, coot and moorhen, on your left.

At the junction a short distance beyond go right to pass under overhead wires as the path levels out. By a footpath finger post stay forward, remaining close to a fence on your right. At the next two footpath signs, maintain direction. At the fourth sign, however, turn left onto a path which passes through some newly planted hawthorns and approaches Shire Brook at a point where it is bridged. This area is known as Penny Loaf. Do not cross the footbridge. Instead turn left so that the Shire Brook is on your right, the slope beyond being covered with willows and the immediate area blessed with hawthorn, brambles and nettles.

Pass beneath more overhead wires before reaching a junction. Turn right to cross a white footbridge over the brook and then climb for a short distance until meeting Stone Lane. Cross directly to a flight of steps but do not climb them.

Instead turn left along the footpath which is separated from the lane itself by a hedgerow. A former sewage works, which once straddled the lane, is in process of being reclaimed as this section of the valley is under development as a recreation and wildlife area.

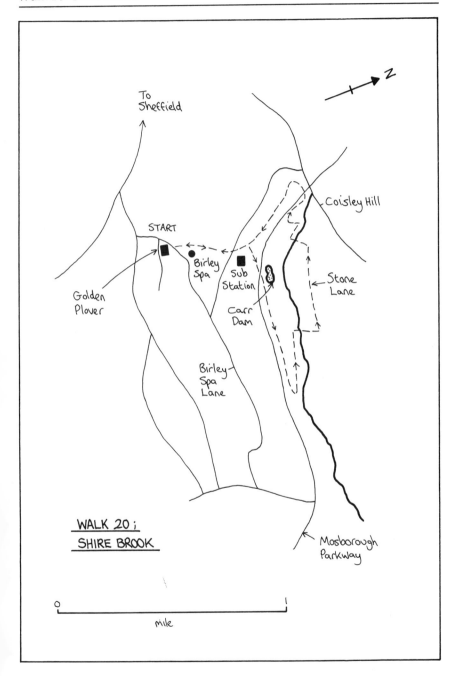

To
Sheffield

Z

Coisley Hill

START

Golden
Plover

Birley
Spa

Sub
Station

Stone
Lane

Carr
Dam

Birley
Spa
Lane

WALK 20;
SHIRE BROOK

Mosborough
Parkway

0   1

mile

At the next junction, recognised by a three-armed signpost, continue along the path but, by the first houses on the right, turn left, cross Stone Lane and take the signed footpath. This drops steeply through an area of bramble, hawthorn, rowan and spiraea where orange tip butterflies proliferate in spring.

Cross the footbridge spanning the Shire Brook and immediately turn right to walk alongside the stream. At the next junction, with another footbridge adjacent to your right, make an acute left turn to another T-junction. Turn right, cross another footbridge after 100 yards and climb slightly to emerge by the traffic island at the junction of Mosborough Parkway and Coisley Hill.

Turn left and, exercising extreme caution, cross the Parkway before making another left turn immediately onto a signed footpath which leads to a T-junction. Turn left, cross a footbridge and climb towards an incongruous-looking street lamp set into the middle of a field. By this, turn left for 20 yards to a Y-junction.

Fork right up the slope to follow a footpath running along the top of a small ridge parallel to the Mosborough Parkway which is on your left. Stay with this for some distance until it loses height to a T-junction by a subway under the Parkway. Do not go under the Parkway but turn right to follow your outward route back to the Golden Plover and a well earned glass of liquid refreshment.

Walk 21. The Ridgeway

Using the Supertram, this walk commences on the outskirts of Sheffield's southern suburbs to follow field paths and bridleways through the undulating cultivated and wooded countryside on the city's boundary with Derbyshire.

Route: The Old Harrow – Carterhall Farm – Ryall's Wood – Litfield Farm – Ridgeway – Birdfield Farm – Birley Lane – Old Harrow.

Start: The Old Harrow Ale House, Whitelane End. Map reference 393829.

Distance: 4½ miles

Maps: 1. "Sheffield", number 743 in the Ordnance Survey's "Pathfinder" series. 2. "Aughton and Carlton in Lindrick", number 744 in the Ordnance Survey's "Pathfinder" series.

Public Transport: The start is served by Supertram and frequent buses (several routes) from the Sheffield Interchange.

By Car: From the city centre take the A6102 to the roundabout where Ridgeway Road becomes Norton Avenue. Turn left along White Lane to the Old Harrow. Alternatively, leave the A6102 at City Road and follow the A616 to Birley Moor where a right turn along Birley Lane leads to the Old Harrow.

Refreshments: There is a cafe at the Ridgeway Cottage Industry Centre (a short diversion from the route). The Old Harrow (see below) serves bar meals.

The Old Harrow Ale House

The Old Harrow, which takes its name from a former nearby farm, occupies a commanding position at the junction of High Lane and White Lane in Base Green, almost on the boundary between Sheffield and Derbyshire. Supertram passes the front door.

It is an imposing modern red-brick building which offers something of a surprise when you pass through its portals. The bar has been simulated to have the appearance of an old cruck barn with lots of exposed brickwork, plain wainscoting, thick wooden beams, wooden floor and a raised area partitioned-off by ranch style fencing. As its name implies it is an ale house offering cask conditioned Whitbread's Trophy Bitter, Castle Eden Bitter and Boddington's Bitter. Bar food is available.

Opening Times: Mondays to Saturdays 11.00 a.m. to 11.00 p.m.; Sundays 12.00 a.m. to 3.00 p.m. and 7.00 p.m. to 10.30 p.m.

The Old Harrow

The Route

From the Old Harrow Ale House cross the tram track and turn left into White Lane, heading in the direction signed to Mosborough village and Eckington.

After about 150 yards, and by the road junction sign, turn right onto a surfaced private road which immediately bends right towards a farm. Within three yards of leaving the road, strike out along the clear, well-walked path which leaves the left-hand side of the farm road to descend gently down the slope of a cultivated field.

The path runs in a perfectly straight line to cross a small wooden footbridge set into the facing hedgerow in the valley bottom. From the far end it climbs, once again as straight as an arrow, to negotiate a wooden squeezer stile and reach Carterhall Lane which is in Derbyshire. Turn left, soon passing Carter Lodge on your left and a very attractive creeper-covered stone cottage on your right, as the lane, flanked by hedgerows, loses height.

Immediately before a cattle grid turn left, as directed by a waymarker post, to pass through a double line of trees to reach a small facing concrete barrier flanked by a small gate on the left-hand side and a stone step stile on the right. Through or over one of these, advance 20 yards

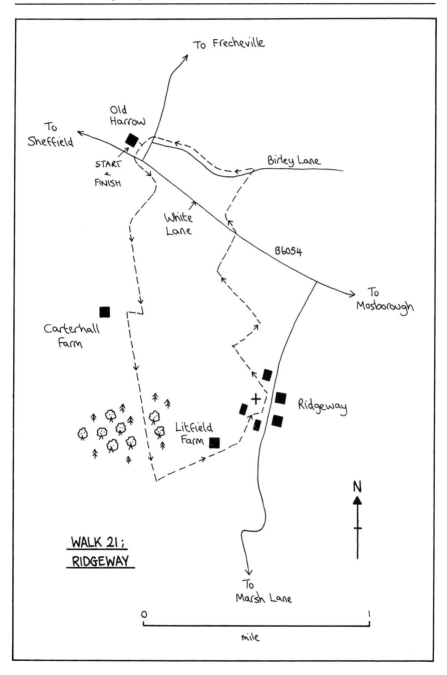

To Frecheville

Old Harrow

To Sheffield

START & FINISH

Birley Lane

White Lane

B6054

To Mosborough

Carterhall Farm

+

Ridgeway

Litfield Farm

WALK 21;
RIDGEWAY

N

To Marsh Lane

0   1
mile

to a waymarker. Ignore the path leading off to the left. Instead continue forwards to a wooden stile alongside a wooden gate. At this point, some 250 yards to your right, is the impressive looking Carterhall Farm.

Over the stile continue along the same line of direction while climbing gradually to the left of a hedge for approximately 30 yards.

As the hedge corners away sharply to your right, turn with it to reach a waymarker post within a few feet. It has two arrows. Ignore the one pointing you towards Carterhall Farm and also an unsigned path heading towards a decrepit gate. Instead, directed by the other waymarker arrow, roughly maintain your line of direction.

Cross the centre of a grass field towards a hedgerow where, obscured by a somewhat large hawthorn tree, there is a stone step stile alongside a maroon coloured metal gate. Over this stile follow the clear path to the immediate right of a headland as it traverses a large arable field. Soon an embryonic hedgerow appears on your left. It consists of hawthorn, beech, birch and other species. It has been planted recently as part of the Countryside Commission's Hedgerow Scheme.

This is an initiative devised to reinstate some of the hundreds of miles of hedgerows which have been grubbed out over recent decades to facilitate the use of the large machinery needed for modern farming methods. Encouragingly this stretch is already attracting butterflies. At the bottom of the field there is a wooden footpath finger post with four arms. Maintain your line of direction along the bridleway to enter Ryall's Wood, a pleasant mixture of deciduous species which provides welcome shade on a very hot sunny day.

By the next waymarker, after only a few yards, veer left to climb a sunken lane leading into an open field and then follow the clear path with a hedge on your immediate left as you lose height to a T-junction. Turn left along a hedged lane which, after a short climb, descends to Litfield Farm. With the farmhouse on your left, allow the waymarks to guide you along the lane. This now has a concrete surface as it loses height rapidly to a T-junction by a small cluster of stone houses in the valley bottom. Cross the ford and turn left up a private road. Notice the house which has a weather vane in the form of a stag's head.

After 70 yards, and by "Lint Croft" and a waymarker, turn right to cross a small bridge with black metal railings. Climb the very steep, stepped path where, at intervals, someone has provided welcome seats.

Eventually the path levels, twists along a driveway for a short distance and passes the "Old School Room" and parish church of St. John the Evangelist before reaching the main road through the village of Ridgeway.

Turn left along the road for a short distance. Pass the entrance to the

"Old Vicarage" on your right. By the far corner of Ridgeway School, built by public subscription in 1823 and now a Methodist Church, turn left into a wide lane recognised by the footpath sign pointing to Robinbrook Lane.

By a white gate veer left onto a narrower path, as shown by a waymarker, to stay outside the boundary wall of the large house on your right. In the far distance ahead is the distinctive concrete water tower at Norton, near Graves Park, while the path itself is lined with lush vegetation consisting of ragwort, bramble, rosebay willowherb, nettles, tall grass and hawthorn which, in high summer, proves attractive to scores of brown and white butterflies.

The path at this point also offers a wide ranging panorama over a rolling and folded arable landscape with the moors of the Peak District clearly visible on a fine day. Closer to hand are some of the conspicuous tower blocks which are one of the hallmarks of post-war Sheffield.

Soon the path reverts to a wider track but, by the first bend, turn right onto an unsigned path which has become almost obscured by the overgrown hedge. Pass a small wooden fence post in the middle of the hedge as you bend low to negotiate a tunnel through the vegetation. The path quickly rises to a metal stile after approximately 100 yards. Over this turn sharp right to a wooden squeezer stile after a mere five yards.

Turn right again and, staying to the immediate left of the hedge, climb a large arable field. Pass beneath overhead power lines and negotiate two further stiles before climbing a very steep but short stretch.

At the top of the field swing left along a broader track to a wooden stile by a metal five-barred gate. Continue forward to the left of a field fence to reach a small open area. Cross this but, immediately in front of a hedge, turn left and so with the hedge on your immediate right, cross a large arable field.

At the far end pass through a gateway which has a wooden post on your left and a stone one on your right. Immediately on your right, and parallel with the path, is a set of double five-barred gates. Pass them and continue for a further five or six yards to an abandoned, galvanised water tank. On entering the next field turn sharp left. Keeping to the right of a hedge turn the first corner, pass a small private woodland on your left and reach the second field corner recognised by a telegraph pole. There, turn left for five yards through the hedge and then turn sharply to the right and, staying to the left of a hedge, advance up the field towards Birdfield Farm, a red-brick house.

In the top right-hand corner of the field, and by a very thick wooden post, veer slightly right to follow the path as it runs between a fence and a hedge. The hedge on the right is eventually replaced by a stone wall while the fence gives way to a hedge.

Finally the path climbs a short flight of steps to White Lane. Cross directly before turning left along the pavement. After 80 yards, and some five yards before a bus stop, turn right up three steps before negotiating a wooden squeezer stile.

The path traverses a field to the left of a fence to reach a stone step stile in the corner. Over this maintain direction to cross a golf course. Keep an eye open for flying golf balls as you climb to the left of a small clump of trees and a short stretch of hedge to an official gap in a temporary fence of chestnut paling.

Cross directly over the lines of Supertram onto Birley Lane. Using the pavement, turn left. From the 210 contour line there is an extensive panorama of North-East Derbyshire to your left and views of the Sheffield suburbs of Frecheville, Base Green and Gleadless laid out in front.

Descend to the road junction and turn left into Fox Lane which is signed to Norton and Gleadless. After 100 yards enter the Old Harrow for a thirst quencher.

Walk 22. Ford

With excellent bridleways and field paths throughout, this walk climbs high above the Moss Valley before returning alongside the brook to the delightful hamlet of Ford.

Route: Ford – Plumbley – West Mosborough – Bowercinder Hill – Neverfear Dam – Ford

Start: The Bridge Inn, Ford. Map reference 402803.

Distance: 4 miles.

Map: "Aughton and Carlton in Lindrick", number 744 in the Ordnance Survey's "Pathfinder" series.

Public Transport: Daily buses from Sheffield Interchange Mondays to Saturdays. No service on Sundays.

By Car: The start of the walk may be reached by Ford Lane which runs from the B6056, Dronfield to Eckington road, at Marsh Lane to the B6054, Mosborough to Sheffield road, at High Lane. There is an official car park for the picnic site adjacent to the Bridge Inn.

Refreshments: The Bridge Inn at Ford and the Wheel at West Mosborough both serve bar meals at lunch times and in the evenings.

The Bridge Inn

The Bridge Inn occupies a prominent position by the River Moss and undoubtedly developed because the tiny hamlet of Ford, as its name implies, was an important crossing point in the days before a bridge was constructed. Its exact age is uncertain but, before it became a pub, it was in turn a sickle and then a button factory. This antiquity is reflected in the rectangular bar where the ceiling is supported by thick old beams matched by plasterwork and stonework.

There is an abundance of copper and brassware but one unusual feature is the display of old bottles and the plaques of English kings in medieval costume. There is also a jousting knight on horseback. Landlord Jim Robinson offers the thirsty walker a choice of cask-conditioned Stone's Traditional Bitter, Boddington's Bitter and Smith's Bitter plus a guest beer which, when I called, was Castle Eden. These are supplemented by Carling Black Label and other lagers, Murphy's Irish Stout and a rare old selection of malt whiskies. An enterprising and changing

The Bridge Inn

menu of bar meals is served every lunch time and every evening except Sundays and Mondays.

Opening Times: Monday to Saturday, 12.00 a.m. to 3.30 p.m. and 7.00 p.m. to 11.00 p.m.; Sundays, 12.00 a.m. to 3.00 p.m. and 7.00 p.m. to 10.30 p.m.

Ford and The Moss Valley

For more than two centuries the Moss Valley was an important industrial area. Although few remains are now to be seen apart from two small dams, there are reminders in such names as Plumbley which means "an open area used for smelting" and Bowercinder Hill. Coal extracted using drift mines and the remains of an old tramway used for transporting this are to crossed in the course of this walk.

The inhabitants of Ridgeway (see Walk 21), Eckington and Mosborough harnessed the water power of the river for driving their simple sickle making machinery.

The people of Ford combined sickle making with farming to eke out a livelihood. Early in the eighteenth century Thomas Cowley was a noted Ford sicklesmith. By the eighteenth century the trade was dominated by the Staniforth family who worked there from the outbreak of

Ford

the Civil War in 1642 until about 1800. Another notable Ford family during the same period was the Turners. A careful look at several houses in the hamlet will reveal their eighteenth century origins.

Bridle Stile, a lane used on this route, was an ancient trackway linking Mosborough with High Lane across an enormous open field known as Ridgeway Field. A careful look at the fields to the north shows that they are long and narrow, a relic of the old Open Field system of farming practised before the eighteenth century Enclosure Movement.

Neverfear Dam, according to local tradition, acquired its unusual name because some men saw a ghost in the vicinity. Afraid at first, they were re-assured when the spirit uttered the words, "Never fear".

The Route

Leave the picnic site car park by passing the toilets on your right to reach Ford Lane. Turn right along the road, climbing steeply in the direction of Ridgeway.

By the 40 mph signs turn right onto a bridleway which is signed with the Mosborough Country Walk logo which features the "Mosborough Mouse". Lined with rosebay willowherb, hedge parsley, bluebells,

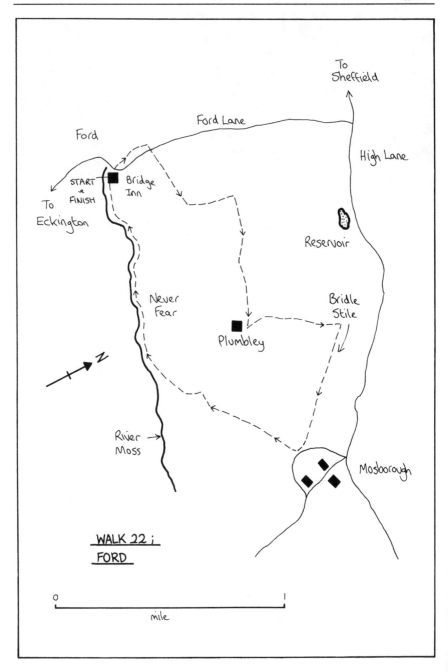

To Sheffield

Ford Lane

Ford

High Lane

START & FINISH

Bridge Inn

To Eckington

Reservoir

Never Fear

Bridle Stile

Plumbley

N

River Moss

Mosborough

WALK 22 ;
FORD

0

mile

hawthorn and elder, the lane runs along the contour while offering some attractive views over steeply rolling countryside dotted with woodlands.

On reaching a footpath finger post with two arms, ignore the paths running off to your left. Instead stay with the lane as it curves to the right but, after a further 10 yards, and by another sign, turn left over a stile to climb steeply through a large meadow with a wall-cum-fence-cum-hedgerow on your right.

Ahead is a prominent ridge while to your left is Ridgeway church. In the field corner negotiate a wooden stile, turn to the right and, with a hedge now on your left, walk for approximately 100 yards before embarking on another climb with a view over the Moss Valley with Ford nestling in the hollow below.

By the field corner swing right for 100 yards of level walking before veering left up the steep slope covered with bracken, heather and gorse. The path is exceptionally clear as it crests the ridge to pass the remnants of a stile made redundant by the removal of a hedgerow.

Continue forward along another distinct path through the centre of a large arable field with skylarks, swallows and house martins as your summer companions.

Descend gradually to a wooden stile, cross a narrow stream and maintain direction with a fence on your left to a wooden stile after 60 yards. Beyond this stay forward to the left of a farm to reach the junction of Plumbley Lane with Plumbley Wood Lane.

Turn left into Plumbley Wood Lane but, after 100 yards and by a white metal five-barred gate and a footpath sign, turn right over a stone step stile. Follow the clear path through a cultivated field while passing beneath overhead power lines and through a gateway before crossing a second field to a tiny copse of deciduous trees.

Follow the path through these and then, staying close to the right-hand field boundary, climb fairly steeply towards two wooden pylons. Your reward is an extensive panorama of North East Derbyshire. On the crest of the ridge continue straight ahead for a completely contrasting vista embracing Mosborough and parts of the City of Sheffield.

By the next footpath sign turn right along Bridle Stile, an ancient trackway. After passing through two rows of trees the lane degenerates into a footpath as it traverses a large open field. However, beyond a football pitch, it reverts to a lane before passing the Fire Station to meet Queen Street in Mosborough directly opposite to Elim Gospel Church.

Turn right into Plumbley Hall Road and follow it round to The Wheel public house. There, by a footpath sign, turn left, and pass in front of the pub to Plumbley Hall Lane. Turn right for 10 yards and then left into Marsh Close. Immediately, and by a footpath sign, turn right to follow the clear path through the centre of a cultivated field.

At the far end of the field turn sharp left and, staying just to the right of a hedge, descend another field to a corner. Turn right again but, where the hedge on your left ends, veer slightly to the right to a wooden stile.

Turn left down a sunken lane, the track of the former railway used for transporting coal. At the first T-junction after 100 yards turn right. After a further five yards veer left over a wooden stile to cross a field corner before meeting the field boundary and staying alongside it with the River Moss audible but not visible on your left and Bowercinder Hill away to your right.

In spring the hedgerow on your left is alive with bluebells, red campion, hedge parsley and celandine. These attract scores of butterflies. After a short distance the path starts a very gentle climb but, by a decrepit five-barred gate turn left over a wooden stile to enter Cadman Wood, a mixture of sweet chestnut, holly, oak and sycamore.

The path loses height rapidly until reaching a T-junction by the river bank. Turn right and, after 20 yards, negotiate a metal stile. Maintain direction along a very broad path which soon passes to the left of Neverfear Dam. From this point onwards the well maintained path wanders across riverside meadows which are transformed into fields of gold by thousands of buttercups during the summer months.

Turn right over a waymarked wooden stile but then resume your direction down some steps and over a footbridge close to a large black pipe. After the next stile proceed to the left of the Mill Pond with its anglers to reach the car park from where you started. If thirsty or in need of food then continue a few extra yards to the Bridge Inn.

Walk 23. Rother Valley

A pleasant easy route following the course of the River Rother and along the Chesterfield Canal. Much of the land has been reclaimed from former industrial workings.

Route: Bedgreave Mill – Killamarsh Meadows – Chesterfield Canal – Norwood – Delves Lane – Bedgreave Mill

Start: The car park, Bedgreave Mill, Rother Valley Country Park. Map reference 454827. An alternative start for those using public transport is The Angel Inn, on the A618 (Mansfield Road) in Norwood. Map reference 468819.

Distance: 4¼ miles.

Map: "Aughton and Carlton in Lindrick", number 744 in the Ordnance Survey's "Pathfinder" series.

Public Transport: The Angel Inn and the main entrance to the Rother Valley Country Park (more than one mile from Bedgreave Mill) are served by regular daily buses from Sheffield Interchange, Rotherham (not Sundays) and Mansfield.

By Car: The main entrance to the Rother Valley Country Park and the Angel Inn are both on the A618, Mansfield Road, between Killamarsh and Wales Bar.

Refreshments: The Angel Inn, Norwood, serves bar meals. The cafe at the Visitor Centre, Bedgreave Mill, Rother Valley Country Park, is open for snacks and light meals every day (except December 25th) from 10.00 a.m. to 5.00 p.m.

Museums: Bedgreave Mill, Rother Valley Country Park. Open daily (except Christmas Day), 10.00 a.m. to 6.00 p.m. Phone – Sheffield (01742) 471452.

The Angel

With its large bar subdivided into smaller sections the Angel has a modern atmosphere with its carpets, banquette seating and low ceilings. Its white exterior makes it a prominent landmark on the Mansfield Road.

Landlord Melvyn Jackson offers a warm and friendly reception matched by a wide range of beers including Whitbread's Trophy,

Whitbread's Bitter, Whitbread's Goldings, Flower's Bitter, Eden Bitter, Adnam's Southwold, Wadworth Brewery's 6X, and Boddington's. There is an equally impressive list of lagers, all on hand pump, including Stella Artois and Heineken's supplemented by Guinness and Murphy's Stout. The walls are decorated by some very tasteful paintings of canal and river scenes reminiscent of works by Constable. These are matched by old photographs of the area.

Opening Times: Mondays to Saturdays, 11.00 a.m. to 11.00 p.m.; Sundays 12.00 a.m. to 3.00 p.m. and 7.00 p.m. to 10.30 p.m.

The Rother Valley

It is so easy to dismiss this area to the south-east of Sheffield's boundary as of little significance, yet it is full of historical interest. Roman remains have been discovered at Killamarsh while that great Roman road, Ryknield Street passed through the district on its way from Cirencester to York. In the succeeding centuries of the so-called "Dark Ages" the area was occupied by Anglo-Saxons who produced such place names as "Chinewoldsmaresc", now rendered as " Killamarsh", and "Walh" meaning "Briton" or "Welshman" or "Foreigner" which has been corrupted into "Wales". The parish church of St. Giles in Killamarsh still boasts a Saxon cross.

Based on the evidence of place names, a case has been put forward for the famous Battle of Brunanburgh in 937 having been fought in the vicinity between the victorious Athelstan of Mercia and Wessex and the combined armies of Scotland, Northumbria and Ireland. "Bedgreave" is interpreted as "Bed Grave" while "Birley" is "Burgh Law" meaning "a burial ground near a fort". Both Killamarsh and nearby Beighton are mentioned in Domesday Book and the church in Killamarsh has traces of Norman stonework.

During the late eighteenth century the Chesterfield Canal was built to link the town with the River Trent thereby facilitating the bulk transport of coal and other products. Today, it is unused but there are plans to re-open stretches for leisure navigation.

The Rother Valley Country Park lies within the boundaries of Rotherham and was developed from a large open-cast coal mining site before being opened to the public in 1983. It is based around a series of lakes – Meadowgate, Nethermoor, Rother Valley and Northern which are supplied by the River Rother. These have been created to control the flooding which formerly affected the valley. Covering 300 hectares, it is criss-crossed by a network of footpaths, cycling and equestrian routes but the focal point is Bedgreave Mill.

Bedgreave Mill

This is a former corn mill built around 1768 and believed to occupy the site of several earlier mills. It initially used water power but this gave way to steam which, in turn, was replaced by an internal combustion engine. Much of the nineteenth century machinery has been preserved and restored so that, on certain days, visitors may see it in operation. A Visitor Centre has been developed at the mill which, apart from providing information, houses an exhibition on the history and natural history of the surrounding area. The park also caters for a wide range of outdoor activities including orienteering, fishing, riding, cycling and various types of water sports.

Further information on the Rother Valley Country Park may be obtained by ringing Sheffield (01742) 471452.

The Route

Leave the Bedgreave Mill complex by crossing the bridge with white railings which spans the River Rother, canalised at this point as part of a flood control scheme. At the far end turn right to walk to the left of the river with its large numbers of wild swans, mallard and other waterfowl.

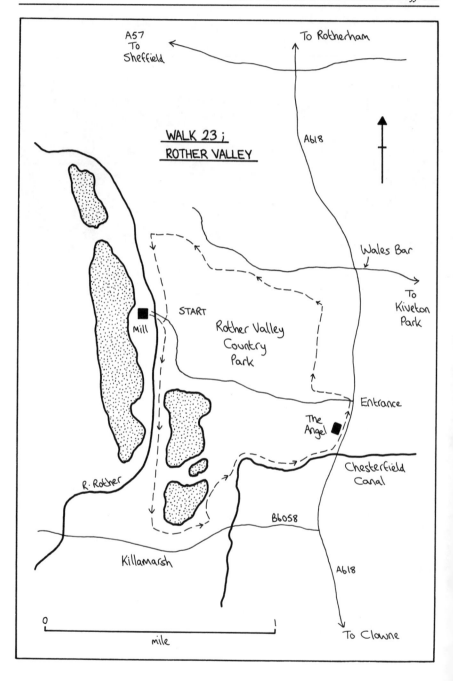

A57
To
Sheffield

To Rotherham

WALK 23 ;
ROTHER VALLEY

A618

Wales Bar

To
Kiveton
Park

START

Mill

Rother Valley
Country
Park

Entrance

The
Angel

Chesterfield
Canal

R. Rother

B6058

Killamarsh

A618

0   1

mile

To Clowne

With views westwards to Waterthorpe and Westfield, the grass path soon diverges from the road to follow the river bank to a wooden sign indicating a path to Killamarsh. Continue in the same direction but now with a fenced-off nature reserve on your left before emerging from the trees to look down on Meadowgate Lake.

This is the focus of the Meadowgate Ornithological Project, funded by British Coal, which is currently studying the birdlife of the lake and its surroundings to collect information which may be used in the future restoration of land disturbed by open-cast mining.

At the time of writing various ornithological groups involved in the survey have recorded 158 species of birds including black-necked grebe, ruddy shelduck, Egyptian goose, osprey, buzzard, glaucous gull and wood sandpiper. More common birds to be found there are cuckoo, mallard, coot, moorhen, lapwing, golden plover, swallow and king-fisher.

Some 250 yards beyond a seat, where the well-maintained path curves round to the right, stay forward, walking along the grass shore to the immediate right of the next lake, Nethermoor. By a small, square red-brick building and a lifebuoy station, fork right along a grass path for a 10 yard climb to a T-junction.

Turn left along the new path which stays a few feet higher than the lake which is now on your left and some 50 yards distant from it until forming a junction with a broad track by a wooden five-barred gate with a smaller gate and a wooden stile adjacent.

Do not use either of these. Instead turn left for 30 yards to a wooden finger post. Ignore the paths signed to Killamarsh and Waleswood. Rather, turn right over a wooden stile to climb a somewhat muddy path with duckboards in places while staying to the right of a fence and a hedge.

Half way up the small field curve through 45 degrees to the right before walking beneath overhead power lines to a stone step stile. Over that maintain direction to pass a pylon after a few yards and then continue for a similar distance to emerge onto the towpath of the Chesterfield Canal. Turn left. The towpath forms part of the Cuckoo Way, a medium distance route which links Chesterfield with the River Trent. At this point the canal has been allowed to dry-out so that only pools of brackish water remain but nature is reclaiming it for its own with hawthorn, elder, alder, willow and other trees rising from the bed.

After passing a small industrial estate on the right, mercifully screened by trees, the path emerges through a gap in a fence onto Bailey Drive. Maintain direction along this road for a few yards and then, staying to the right of two small brick built factories and still to the left of the canal fence, walk along a lane for 100 yards until meeting the A618 at Norwood. Turn left for a welcome pint at the Angel. After refreshments, resume walking along the A618 in the direction of Wales Bar. Soon you will pass from Derbyshire into Yorkshire when crossing County Dyke.

Some 250 yards after leaving the Angel turn left into the main entrance of the Rother Valley Country Park for a little peace and quiet after the noise and bustle of that short distance along the main road.

By the entrance kiosk and a footpath finger post, turn right through a small gate bearing a yellow waymarker arrow to take the path signed to Waleswood. Ahead in the distance lies an enormous looking hill. Do not worry: it is not for climbing. It is a colliery slag heap now grassed over to blend with the remaining restored landscape.

Walk through a hay meadow with a ditch and wire fence on your right. In the first field corner, where a wooden fence commences and with a wooden pylon some 40 yards to the left, ignore a wooden stile on your right. Instead, negotiate a facing wooden stile to pass between some newly-planted trees while staying to the left of a fence with wooden stables and grazing horses in the paddock beyond.

Cross a wooden footbridge to a waymarker post, swing left to a second post after 20 yards, and then bend to the right as the path embarks on a gentle climb. Ignoring another stile on the right, continue climbing for a further 20 yards to yet another waymarker.

There turn towards the left and, walking under more overhead wires, maintain your upwards direction until reaching a prominent yellow waymark on the corner post of a fence. Turn left so that a wire fence is on your right. Stay alongside this fence for a considerable distance but, where it corners by a five-barred gate and a waymark, turn sharp right for four yards to reach a wide, chatter track. Turn left along this to a footpath finger post at the junction with Delves Lane at the very foot of that formidable looking slag heap and by one of those former white telephone exchanges which are now redundant.

Taking your direction from the footpath sign, head towards Bedgreave Mill, still climbing along the track as it veers away from Delves Lane. Ignore a footpath sign and stile on your right on the crest of the rise. Stay with your track for views of the Rother Valley Lake directly ahead as it begins a twisting descent which ultimately brings you to the main surfaced road through the country park.

Turn right for 100 yards and then left over the bridge with white railings to regain Bedgreave Mill.

Walk 24. Conisborough

Another route using bridleways and field paths through a mainly arable landscape but visiting a quiet wild oasis centred around a group of tiny reservoirs.

Route: Hill Top Hotel – Firsby Hall Farm – Firsby Reservoirs – Ravenfield Grange – Conisborough Grange – Park Lane – Hill Top Hotel.

Start: Hill Top Hotel, Conisborough. Map reference 495975.

Distance: 7 miles.

Map: "Rotherham", number 727 in the Ordnance Survey's "Pathfinder" series.

Public Transport: The start is served by frequent daily buses from Doncaster, Rotherham and Sheffield.

By Car: The Hill Top Hotel is on the A630(T) which is the main road between Rotherham and Doncaster. There is a car park at the hotel and off road parking nearby.

Refreshments: The Hill Top Hotel serves bar meals.

The Hill Top Hotel

The Hill Top Hotel lives up to its name, standing on the crest of the steep hill which separates the villages of Conisborough and Hooton Roberts. Surprisingly, in view of its position in this area, its sign depicts a rambler complete with rucksack on his back. Landlady Ellen Sapey has no idea how this particular symbol came to be chosen or, indeed, who chose it. But, as you will see if you choose to follow this route, the countryside around does make for some pleasant rambling.

What is not surprising is the warm welcome extended by Ellen. The bar is noted for its thick wooden beams and exposed plasterwork, the walls being adorned by a miscellaneous collection of coaching lamps, harness, kettles, plates, brassware and hunting horns in all shapes and sizes. All these create a genuine olde-worlde atmosphere.

There is a good selection of bar meals from sandwiches to Ploughman's, scampi, filled Yorkshire Puddings and gammon. They are served at lunch time and in the evenings. Liquid refreshments include cask-conditioned Mansfield Bitter and Riding Traditional Bitter plus Guinness and a selection of lagers.

Opening Times: Mondays to Saturdays, 11.30 a.m. to 2.30 p.m. and 4.30 p.m. to 11.00 p.m.; Sundays, 12.00 a.m. to 3.00 p.m. and 7.00 p.m. to 10.30 p.m.

Hill Top Hotel

Firsby Reservoirs

Firsby Reservoirs provide a small yet apparently remote wilderness oasis in the centre of a predominantly arable area of countryside. They consist of two areas of water created in the 1870s by Doncaster Corporation to act as holding reservoirs for the new one then under construction at nearby Thrybergh. They are connected to Thrybergh by two conduits. A sluice gate for one of these is still visible at the smaller of Firsby's two reservoirs.

They passed into the possession of Rotherham Metropolitan Borough Council in 1980 from the Yorkshire Water Authority, now Yorkshire Water PLC. They are managed essentially as a quiet wildlife area where the public may relax in peace and solitude.

Both lakes have paths round them and benches have been provided. The open area of water is gradually decreasing as the lakes silt up and are quickly colonised by new plants such as willow, gorse and broom. Other flowers on the site include wild mint and honeyed meadowsweet.

The flowers attract a range of butterflies, the most notable being small tortoiseshell, peacock and red admiral. Birds either visiting or breeding there according to season include the little grebe, kestrel, swift and swallow not to mention a range of woodland birds from blue tit to blackbird, thrush and yellowhammer.

Conisborough Castle

Often neglected because of its position in the centre of the urbanised area of South Yorkshire, Conisborough Castle is one of the finest buildings in the care of English Heritage. Its circular keep, visible throughout much of this walk, is the oldest in England. After being exposed to the elements for decades, if not centuries, the keep has been re-roofed and new internal floors installed for conservation purposes in 1994. So, today the castle has much of its original appearance. Dating from the eleventh century, it occupies a strategic position above the River Don.

It was also used as the setting for scenes in Sir Walter Scott's novel, "Ivanhoe" and his descriptions provide a realistic idea of that the surrounding countryside looked like before industrialisation crept through the valley. It also has an extensive range of outer bailey walls. There is a Visitor Centre and, during summer months, the interior grounds are used for medieval-style tournaments.

Opening Times: 1st April to 30th September, daily from 10.00 a.m. to 6.00 p.m.; 1st October to 31st March, Tuesday to Sunday, 10.00 a.m. to 4.00 p.m. Closed Mondays.

Ravenfield Park

This is the remnant of a private deer park owned by the Westby family who lived there for several centuries. It was enclosed during the eighteenth century when the hall was built and the formal gardens laid out. Between 1749 and 1820 ownership changed several times but Walter Osborne, who lived there between 1766 and 1788, was responsible for enlarging the hall and creating a new system of ponds and watercourses.

In 1972 the park was sold to the Phoenix Social and Sporting Club to provide angling facilities. Since then, in association with Rotherham Metropolitan Borough Council, the quality of the fishing has been improved and concessionary footpaths have been created to allow access by members of the general public.

The Route

From the Hill Top Hotel cross the A630 into the facing signed bridleway, passing between a farm on the left and the modernised Toll Bar House on the right. The wide lane, although hedged on both sides, offers extensive views over the arable fields. Where the hedgerows terminate, the lane bends through 45 degrees to the left before embarking on a gentle descent through verges which are lined with poppies during the summer months.

A short distance before reaching Firsby Hall Farm the tracks swings to the right and then to the left so that it follows a course just to the left of the farm buildings. A very short distance beyond these, veer round to the right as the lane passes below a canopy of trees for 100 yards before reaching a notice which reads, "Firsby Reservoirs".

After a short break to absorb the atmosphere continue along the main track with a wall on the right initially and then flanking both sides as the bridleway climbs beneath another tree canopy to pass the entrance to Ravenfield Park on the right.

Ignore a footpath sign, also on the right, instead continuing to climb gradually along Arbour Lane and passing under a former railway bridge to reach the point where the lane turns through 90 degrees to the right to become Garden Lane. At this point, and by a footpath finger post, leave the surfaced lane to maintain your direction along an unsurfaced one flanked by hedgerows as it continues climbing until emerging onto arable land where the skylark announces its presence in season.

As the lane levels out it develops into an ordinary footpath running along the western boundary of a field to a waymarked stile. Over this, veer slightly left, as directed by the waymark, traverse a pasture by heading towards a pylon on the crest of the facing hill.

On the way, cross a plank footbridge and then, by the pylon, veer further to the left to reach a stile beneath overhead wires. Over the stile maintain your direction over an arable field, pass between two wooden pylon support poles and aim for a distant but clearly visible stile. Beyond that continue in the same direction as you cross a paddock, pass through a hedge gap and go over the next field to the stile alongside a metal five-barred gate and the outbuilding of Ravenfield Grange Farm

This allows an exit onto the road linking Braithwell and Thrybergh at a height of 112 metres above sea level compared with 82 metres at your starting point by the Hill Top Hotel.

Turn left along the road soon passing the boundary sign informing you that your are passing from Rotherham into Doncaster. There is a wide grass verge, ideal for walking as the road crosses Braithwell

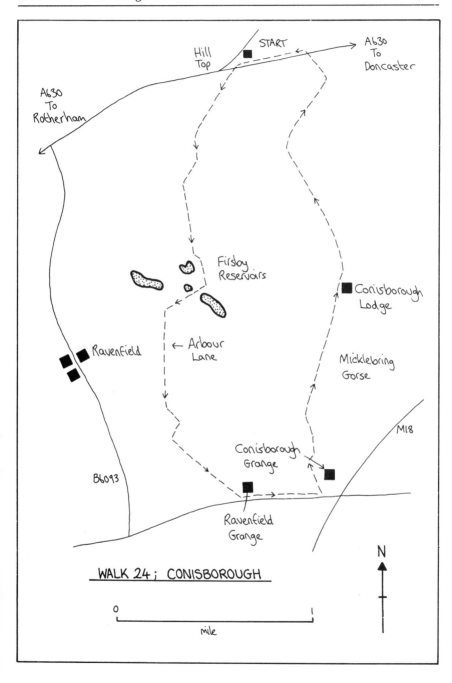

WALK 24; CONISBOROUGH

Common in the direction of the M18 with its ceaseless flow of high speed traffic.

After almost half a mile, and some 100 yards beyond a former railway track now noted for its display of lupins, and opposite a side road signed to Bramley, turn left into a signed bridleway.

The first 100 yards are surfaced but, having kept to the left of Conisborough Grange Farm, it develops into a wide track known as Park Lane. It offers good views in the far distance ahead of Conisborough Castle with its new roof. Pass through a metal five-barred gate, way-marked only on its reverse side, and turn sharp right to follow the indistinct path round the field boundary with a hedge on your right.

Over a stile, continue the same line of direction down the left-hand side of the next field towards a waymarked small wooden gate which allows passage onto a lane, also flanked by hedgerows.

An alternative route is possible. Through the metal gate stay with the track as it drops down the hill. However, just before Birk Hall farm, turn right with a peculiar-shaped tree on your left, to pass through a second five-barred gate. Then, using the waymark as your direction guide, cross a field diagonally to the right. In the field corner you will find the small wooden gate which permits access onto the lane.

Once through this gate cross the culverted Firsby Brook for the start of a steep climb with Micklebring Gorse on your right. Foxgloves decorate the verges while the radio masts on Beacon Hill are away to your right. On the summit a two-armed footpath post stands at a cross roads in the path network. Ignore the paths running to the left and the right, continuing along Park Lane until reaching an unsigned Y-junction. Fork right to pass to the left of Conisborough Lodge Farm.

By the next footpath sign, once again ignore a path to the right, instead maintaining your direction. Notice the lumps in the field on your left. These are marked on the Ordnance Survey Map as "Air Shafts", probably from a former coal mine.

After some distance Park Lane is joined by another track coming from Park Farm Cottages on the right. Stay with Park Lane as it bends sharply to the right with views of Conanby and Conisborough appearing ahead and the distinctive white water tower at Warmsworth visible to the right.

Soon the lane reaches the A630. Cross to the pavement and make a left turn for the short distance to the Hill Top Hotel.

Walk 25. High Melton

Starting on a nature reserve, this walk climbs to one of the most attractive villages in South Yorkshire before crossing a prairie to a gruesome spot and returning by a holy well.

Route: Denaby Ings – High Melton – Hangman Stone – St. Helen's Well – The Crown – Barnburgh Grange – Denaby Ings

Start: Car park, Denaby Ings Nature Reserve. Map reference 499011.

Distance: 6 miles.

Map: "Doncaster & Dearne", number 716 in the Ordnance Survey's "Pathfinder" series.

Public Transport: The start has daily buses from Mexborough and Doncaster. High Melton has buses from Mexborough, Doncaster and Barnsley.

By Car: The start is reached by a minor road linking Mexborough with Marr and Cadeby which leaves the A6023 in Mexborough at map reference 488001. In Marr it leaves the A635 at map reference 513052.

Refreshments: The Crown Inn serves bar meals at lunch time and in the evenings.

The Crown Inn

The Crown Inn stands at a minor road junction at the foot of Ludwell Hill on the road linking the villages of Barnburgh and High Melton.

The exterior of this modern pub is a mixture of white rendering and stonework. Inside, although it is obviously modern, there has been an attempt to suggest an atmosphere of days long since departed. The large, open bar has copper-topped tables and there are plush banquettes and turkey carpets. There is also a separate restaurant with its own bar. The walls are decorated with copper frying pans of all sizes, pottery plates and a selection of old prints.

There is an extensive range of bar meals with many daily specials in addition to the standard menu. Beers on offer include Webster's Yorkshire Bitter, John Smith's Bitter, John Smith's Magnet and Courage's Director's Bitter, all on hand pump.

Opening Times: Mondays to Saturday, 11.00 a.m. to 11.00 p.m.; Sundays, 12.00 a.m. to 3.00 p.m. and 7.00 p.m. to 10.30 p.m.

Denaby Ings

Denaby Ings is one of 59 nature reserves belonging to the Yorkshire Wildlife Trust, being established in 1957 with various areas added since including the embankment of the former Dearne Valley Railway. There is a wide spectrum of habitat, the open waters attracting many species of wildfowl while the woodland sections are ideal for woodland birds such as the robin, thrush, blackbird and titmice.

The reserve is also noted for its butterfly and insect population while the meadowland produces an interesting range of flora. Rabbits, field voles, mice and other small mammals are common and this reserve is one of the few places in Yorkshire where it is still possible to see grass snakes.

The history of the reserve can be traced back to Norman times when it is believed that it was the site of a mill on the north bank of the River Dearne. This was given to the Priory of Hampole, near Doncaster, by Avicia de Taini and her daughter, Sibilla de Clairfait in 1153.

Thereafter the site had a chequered history, passing from one family to another until, in 1666 it passed into the Montagu family which retained it until 1927. No fewer than 169 species of bird have been recorded there which is a significant total in view of the fact that the reserve has been created amongst former colliery waste tips and in the centre of a former industrial area.

High Melton Church

The attractive church of St. James in High Melton is one of the oldest in Yorkshire. It was built in 1153 by Avicia de Taini who founded the Priory of Hampole. The ground plan is unusual because there is a short nave with the Chancel and Western Tower and a continuous south aisle which runs the entire length of the church. Until the reign of Richard 11 at the end of the fourteenth century it was dedicated to All Saints. It is built of local limestone with oak roof timbers. Much of the original stonework is still in place.

Barnburgh

Although our route does not pass through the centre of Barnburgh, the village will repay a visit afterwards. According to the records it existed in Saxon times when it belonged to King Osul but after 1066 it passed through a number of families until the Cresacres took possession. Their lordship is reflected in the numerous memorials to the family in the parish church which was built in 1150 of local limestone.

High Melton church

Barnburgh is the setting for the famous Cat and Man legend. According to this, Sir Percival Cresacre was making his way home through Melton woods when he was attacked by a wild cat. The cat unseated him and his mount returned without rider to Barnburgh Hall. Desperately trying to fight off the marauding animal, Sir Percival tried to follow in the same direction as his mount. When he reached the church he was so exhausted he sought sanctuary inside. The animal followed. Sir Percival by this time was beyond all earthly assistance and as he stretched out in his death throes he crushed the cat against the wall. Hence Barnburgh Church is known as "The Cat and Man Church" where the cat killed the man and the man killed the cat.

A later Cresacre, Anna, married John More, the only son of Sir Thomas More and the More family continued to live in Barnburgh Hall until 1820. The medieval dovecote in the grounds of Barnburgh Hall is preserved as a scheduled ancient monument. The Hall itself was demolished in 1970 by the National Coal Board because of subsidence caused by mining.

The Route

From the car park of Denaby Ings Nature Reserve turn right along the road from Mexborough and cross Dearne Bridge to reach the junction between Pasture Road and Pasture Lane. Exercising extreme caution, cross directly to the apex of the junction to a footpath sign which is partially concealed by vegetation.

In the absence of a stile of any description, proceed through the hedge onto a clear, straight footpath traversing a cultivated field with lapwing circling overhead in early summer. During the same season the call of the cuckoo can be heard and, even in broad daylight, so too can the call of the tawny owl.

There are overhead wires running parallel, approximately 50 yards to the left as the path aims directly for the wooded ridge ahead. On reaching the first field boundary, nothing more than a ditch, cross a footbridge and then stay forward, climbing straight up the arable field with an ever expanding view over the Dearne Valley.

To the right it is possible to glimpse the tall, sturdy keep of Conisborough castle with its brand new roof added in 1944 (see Walk 24). As the path reaches higher ground it acquires a golf course to the right and there is an abundance of poppies.

Negotiate a wooden stile before crossing a horse paddock towards a footpath sign alongside a stile. This provides access to Doncaster Road in High Melton, an attractive village of mellow limestone houses.

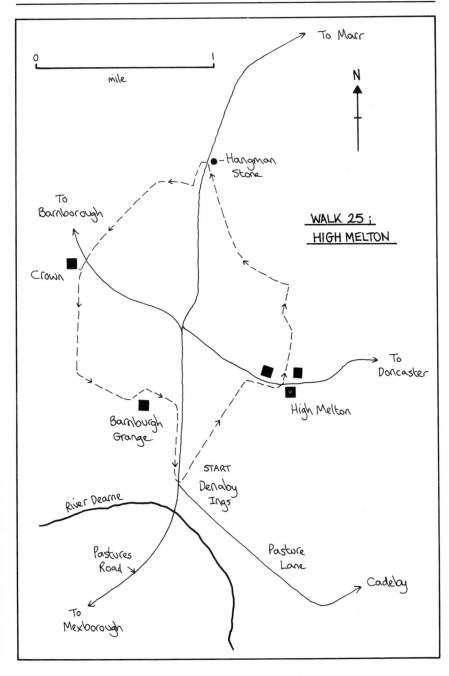

WALK 25 ;
HIGH MELTON

Turn right along the pavement which is wisely separated from the road either by a fence or a stone wall until the main entrance to Doncaster College. By the College, turn left, cross the road and proceed along Hangman Stone Lane, a bridleway signed to Marr. Initially it passes between new houses but, by "Boxtree House", it corners through 90 degrees to the right before passing to the right of "Oakleigh Cottage".

Ignore another lane going off to the left and, by the final house, a strange modern structure of wood, pass through an official fence gap and maintain direction across an enormous arable field. This, no doubt, is the product of considerable hedgerow removal.

To the right is a view towards the Doncaster area while, directly ahead, Melton Wood is in constant sight. The going is absolutely level and it is somewhat reminiscent of walking over an American prairie or through parts of East Anglia.

After half a mile, with the square tower of High Melton church gradually receding into the distance behind, a T-junction is reached by a waymarker post. Turn left for distant views of Hoober Stand (see walk 28) and Greno Woods (see Walk 8). After a further half mile the wide track corners through 90 degrees to the right, still traversing the same field.

After a further considerable distance you pass through a gateway to emerge onto Hangman Stone Road at Hangman Stone. According to local tradition a man stole a sheep in High Melton and was leading it with a rope fastened round his waist. When he reached this point he paused for a rest. Placing the animal on top of a stone, he sat down. The animal slipped off on the far side of the stone so that the rope slipped up around the thief's neck and strangled him. If the legend is correct it was rough justice because the penalty for sheep stealing in those days was hanging.

Turn left along the road ignoring a signed bridleway on the right after a mere 10 yards. Continue downhill with a bank of guelder rose on your left. After 150 yards turn right into St. Helen's Lane, another signed bridleway. This runs level below Barnburgh Cliff which is on your right. After some distance it bends to the left soon passing the site of the former St. Helen's Chapel, of which little now remains above ground.

Suddenly there is a transformation in the landscape. The countryside assumes an undulating appearance with more trees and hedgerows. Ahead is a view of Mexborough, a small town with mining connections which was once an important railway junction in the Don Valley.

Gradually St. Helen's Lane loses height as it develops into a wide, unfenced track. A few yards beyond an abandoned quarry it corners through 90 degrees to the left before reverting to a traditional sunken lane and continuing until its meets the road between Barnburgh and High Melton at the foot of Ludwell Hill.

Cross into the facing minor road signed to Harlington with the Crown Inn standing on the corner. After 200 yards, by a cottage and where the road bends to the right, turn left into Grange Lane which is signed as a public footpath. It is open on either side as it goes over Barnburgh Common, a large expanse of open land lying low beside the River Dearne. Eventually the lane turns left and passes beneath overhead wires as it ascends towards Barnburgh Grange.

Pass between the Grange buildings, staying with the track to meet Melton Mill Road. Turn right along this to the junction of Pastures Road and Pasture Lane before retracing your steps to the car.

Walk 26. Clayton

From a village stricken by the closure of the South Yorkshire coalfield, this route leads us across open countryside to an ancient and attractive village of sandstone houses.

Route: The Thurnscoe – Clayton – Back Lane – Clayton Common – Wink House – Frickley Beck – Stotfold Road – The Thurnscoe.

Start: The Thurnscoe Hotel, Thurnscoe. Map reference 454057

Distance: 5 miles.

Map: "Doncaster & Dearne ", number 716 in the Ordnance Survey's "Pathfinder" series.

Public Transport: The start is served by frequent daily buses from Barnsley, and Doncaster. Frequent buses daily (not Sundays) from Mexborough and Rotherham.

By Car: The start is reached by the B6411 which runs from the A635 (Barnsley to Doncaster road) at Hickleton to Great Houghton. There is parking in side roads close to the Thurnscoe Hotel.

Refreshments: The Thurnscoe Hotel serves bar meals at lunch time and in the evenings. Fish and chip shops in Thurnscoe.

The Thurnscoe Hotel

The Thurnscoe Hotel is a large red brick affair which stands on the main road through this former mining community. As you enter it has a large open bar on the right with a restaurant on the left.

There are wooden tables and plush banquettes in the lounge with its high ceiling which is typical of a pub built between the two World Wars. Decorated with rural scenes and regimental shields, it has cream-coloured walls and ceiling. It also has a snooker room.

Bar meals, selected from an extensive menu, are served in the non-smoking restaurant which is decorated with racing and hunting prints plus a portrait of Queen Elizabeth the Queen Mother. It also serves as the Headquarters of the local British Legion. The Thurnscoe serves Stone's Best Bitter and John Smith's Bitter, both on hand pump.

Opening hours: Mondays to Saturdays, 11.00 a.m. to 11.00 p.m.; Sundays, 12.00 a.m. to 3.00 p.m. and 7.00 p.m. to 10.30 p.m.

Thurnscoe

Until recently Thurnscoe was a thriving mining community but it has been affected by the closure of the South Yorkshire coalfield. Signs of these changes may be observed in the gaunt, silent towers which once housed colliery winding gear, the slag heaps now being reclaimed and the number of pubs that stand empty. Its housing is typical of a mining community, almost all belonging to the late years of the nineteenth century and the early years of the twentieth, mostly in red brick.

Clayton

Although mentioned in Domesday Book, Clayton appears to have avoided contact with the world ever since. The church, mainly Norman, is some distance outside the village and serves the neighbouring village of Frickley as well.

Clayton has preserved its charming rural appearance which belies its geographical situation in the heart of one of Britain's major coalfields. Its sandstone cottages, clustered around a village pond and a handful of farms, would not be out of place in the Cotswolds. It has remained a rural oasis in the heart of an industrial region.

Unusual road name in Clayton

The Route

From the entrance of the Thurnscoe Hotel turn left along Houghton Road, the main road through the village. Just beyond a garage on the left, make a right turn into Merrill Road. Where this bends round to the right, a few yards beyond the entrance into Gooseacre Avenue on your left, and also with a school on your left, turn left onto a path indicated by a vandalised footpath sign.

This path is surfaced initially as it climbs to the left of some houses and to the right of open grassland. Where the path swings to the right towards the houses, fork left onto a wide grass path which passes just to the left of an electricity pylon.

By the last of the houses a Y-junction is reached. Take the left-hand path which means, in effect, maintaining direction a short distance to the right of a row of hawthorns but gradually veering left to meet them.

As the path traces its route through a shallow hollow, the fields slope away upwards on either side with swallows, swifts and other birds flying overhead in early summer. There is also a partially concealed ditch on your left.

In the far corner of the first field you will arrive at a T-junction. Turn left through a hedge gap and cross a footbridge to a second T-junction. Turn right and, staying to the left of a ditch, aim for some tall trees, soon passing some water tanks on your right. 25 yards beyond these turn right over the ditch and then turn sharp left, so maintaining direction along the path but now to the right of both hedge and ditch. In the distance behind, the silent pithead gear of Thurnscoe Colliery is still.

By two large oak trees the path turns left over a wooden stile and then right, as shown by a waymarker. From this point is starts its long but very gradual climb before levelling to pass a children's playground and Old Hall Farm, both on your right. Over a wooden stile, continue forwards between a hedge on your right and a fence on your left until reaching the main road through Clayton village.

Turn right but, by Old Hall Farm turn left into Hall Brig Road to pass several charming stone cottages and farms. Hall Brig becomes Common Lane and, 100 yards beyond the final house, a junction of no fewer than five lanes is reached. Take the first on your right, indicated by a footpath sign. It is very wide but unsurfaced as it passes between hedgerows with a fine view of Frickley Colliery and its massive tip away to your left and the attractive village of Hooton Pagnall in the far distance directly ahead.

Ignore the first footpath sign on your right and pass Wink House Farm on your left. After half a mile cross the main Sheffield to York railway

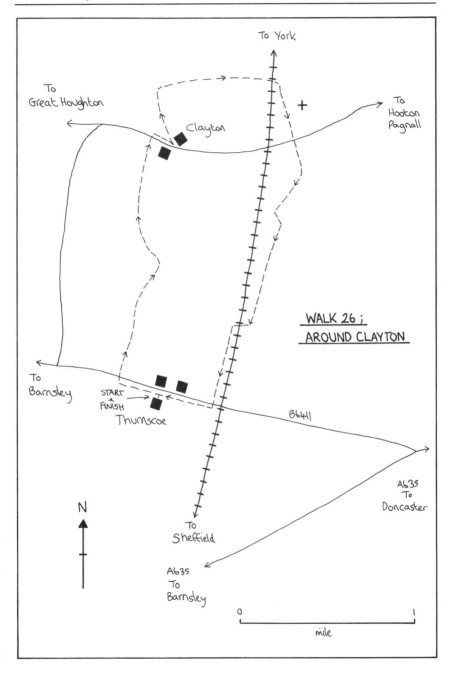

To York

To
Great Houghton

Clayton

To
Hooton
Pagnall

WALK 26 ;
AROUND CLAYTON

To
Barnsley

START
&
FINISH
Thurnscoe

B6411

A635
To
Doncaster

N

To
Sheffield

A635
To
Barnsley

0   1

mile

line by a stone bridge. Just beyond, and by a stone house which stands where the lane bends to the left through 90 degrees, turn right over a small footbridge before negotiating a small wooden waymarked gate.

Stay to the right of the hedge. Where this ends it is replaced by a ditch with Frickley Chapel visible a short distance to the left. Pass through another small wooden gate in a fence, cross Frickley Brook, and stay forward until arriving at Church Field Road, the minor road linking the villages of Clayton and Hooton Pagnall.

Cross directly to a footpath sign showing a bridleway which is little more than a footpath. Follow this noting that the ditch on your left acts as a field boundary.

Aim for a clump of three trees in the distance, two willow, one elder. By these turn right for 10 yards and then turn left over a wooden footbridge before climbing a gentle rise with a short stretch of hawthorn hedge on your right.

Where this ends it is open arable land but the clear, distinctive path aims for a solitary tree with a waymarker post adjacent. These stand at a T-junction formed by the path meeting a lane. Turn left along the track which is known as Stotfold Road. After 50 yards, and by another bridleway sign, turn right onto another broad track flanked by arable fields.

At the cross-roads in the path network, where there is a footpath sign, stay forward for 200 yards and then turn left to walk alongside the railway which is on your right.

On reaching a set of concrete posts turn right over a railway bridge but, at the far end, turn left to walk to the right of the fence alongside the railway. When the path becomes surfaced it swings away from the railway and passes to the right of Thurnscoe station before emerging onto Station Road.

Turn right and stay along the pavement as it becomes Houghton Road. Pass a bowling green on your left before regaining the Thurnscoe Hotel.

Walk 27. Swinton

A short easy walk using woodland and field paths through gentle countryside which has some points of historical interest.

Route: Woodman Inn – Pottery Ponds – Wath Wood – Abdy – Roman Ridge – Blackamoor – Woodman Inn

Start: The Woodman Inn, Swinton. Map reference 443989

Distance: 3 miles.

Map: "Rotherham", number 727 in the Ordnance Survey's "Pathfinder" series.

Public Transport: There are frequent daily buses to the Woodman Inn from Mexborough, Rotherham, Sheffield and Barnsley.

By Car: The Woodman Inn stands on the A633, Rotherham to Wath road, only a few yards from its junction with the B6092, Swinton to Upper Haugh road, and the A6022, the Swinton to Mexborough road. Apart from the pub car park there is a larger one and a picnic site at the Pottery Ponds off the B6092 which is about 200 yards from the Woodman.

Refreshments: Bar meals are available at the Woodman in at lunch time and in the evening.

The Woodman Inn

From the outside, the Woodman Inn appears to be of indeterminate age but inside, the thick wooden beams framing the bar indicate a pub of long standing. The name itself is indicative of forests in the area of which Wath Woods are but the survivors. There is little doubt, either, that the Woodman once slaked the thirst of potters working at the nearby Rockingham Pottery.

There is an antique but no-nonsense air about the wooden-backed settles, wooden tables and wainscoting in the small bar. The walls sport a variety of pictures including a reproduction Gainsborough, and there are various ornaments. One unusual feature is the stone fireplace painted in red with the mortar picked out in black.

Mine hosts, Peter and Yvonne Shakespeare, offer a range of bar food at lunch time and during the evening. This may be washed down with cask conditioned John Smith's Magnet, John Smith's Best Bitter, Webster's Yorkshire Bitter or Beamish Stout, also on draught.

Opening Times: Mondays to Saturdays, 11.00 a.m. to 3.00 p.m. and 6.00 p.m. to 11.00 p.m.; Sundays, 12.00 a.m. to 3.00 p.m. and 7.00 p.m. to 10.30 p.m.

The Woodman

The Rockingham Pottery

The Rockingham Pottery, named after the Marquess of Rockingham of nearby Wentworth Woodhouse, was established in 1745 by Edward Butler. It enjoyed varying fortunes and changed ownership on several occasions, at one period being controlled by the renowned Leeds Pottery. At the height of its fame in the early nineteenth century it employed more than 300 people, a large proportion of the Swinton population.

It enjoyed a period of artistic and commercial success under the ownership of the Brameld family when it obtained large orders from many of the crowned heads of Europe including the Tsars of Russia. Many of these patrons never paid their bills and as a consequence a decline set in.

Help was forthcoming from the Earl Fitzwilliam, a descendant of Lord

Rockingham, but sales were then concentrated on the home market. Even then an order for a comprehensive dinner service from Buckingham Palace resulted in a financial loss and, after a period producing mundane ware, the Rockingham Pottery finally closed down in 1842.

The works were described as "having the facilities for the manufacture of china and earthenware on a very extensive scale". There were two biscuit ovens, five glazing ovens, three enamelling ovens, seven throwing wheels, several hardening kilns for painters and a sliphouse room which could handle 50 tons of clay every week.

The pottery was renowned for its Rockingham ware which rivalled such makes as Wedgwood, Crown Derby and Royal Worcester and even today remains a valuable collector's item. It was creamware dipped in a brown manganese oxide stained glaze which was produced from 1785 until 1842. Other specialities were the Cadogan teapots and brown glazed Toby Jugs.

The Route

Leaving the Woodman Inn walk for about 100 yards down Warren Vale Road, the A633, towards the large traffic roundabout at the junction with the B6092, Blackamoor Road, and the A6022. By the island turn right into Blackamoor Road but, after a further 100 yards, make a right turn through a wooden kissing gate and then advance another 30 yards through the picnic area to a second kissing gate.

Beyond this veer slightly left over the grass towards a stone wall and, keeping to the right of this, walk towards the Pottery Ponds. Allow time for an inspection of the kiln and other relics on the site.

Re-join the path and follow it between the two ponds to a green metal kissing gate before climbing a short distance to re-join Warren Vale Road. Turn left. Pass the entrance to Wath Wood Drive but, immediately, turn left along a signed path running parallel to Wath Wood Drive which is on your left. There are houses on your right.

100 yards beyond "Gilton Hose", a large red brick affair, pass between a set of metal posts and then a wooden squeezer stile to enter Wath Woods. Almost at once, turn right along a charming woodland path which clings to the contour as it wends its way through the mixed deciduous trees. Stay with the main path, ignoring several unofficial ones on both sides.

Descend a very steep but short stretch and then climb. At the top of the rise, with a wall on your right, turn left to remain with the path as it undulates until leaving the woods through a barrier to meet the road to Wath Wood Hospital. Many years ago this was an isolation hospital

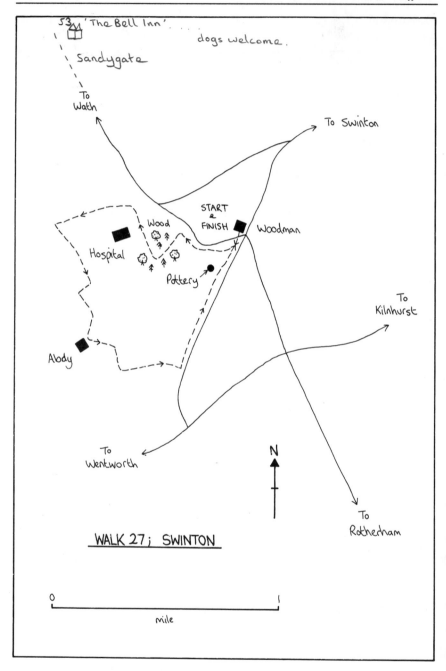

53 'The Bell Inn'   dogs welcome.

Sandygate

To
Wath

To Swinton

START
&
FINISH

Wood

Woodman

Hospital

Pottery

To
Kilnhurst

Abdy

To
Wentworth

N

To
Rotherham

WALK 27; SWINTON

0   1

mile

specialising in diphtheria and scarlet fever but, subsequently, was transformed into a small general hospital.

Cross the road directly into a lane signed as a public footpath. Lose height for 100 yards but, by the next footpath sign, veer slightly to the right over a stone step stile to walk to the left of a fence and to the right of a hedge.

Pass through a metal barrier into a field of lupins with the hospital to your left. After a second metal barrier and by Wath Wood Houses, the path forms a T-junction with a lane. Turn left and advance just beyond a dilapidated and unsightly corrugated metal fence to a footpath sign by a junction.

Make a left turn onto a field path and follow the boundary in the direction of the hospital. However, by the first corner, swing right to walk parallel with some overhead wires across an arable field into a shallow valley.

In the bottom right-hand corner of the field negotiate a stile and advance to the left of a telegraph pole to a gap in a tall hawthorn hedge. Through the gap, maintain the line of direction over a meadow full of buttercups in early summer until reaching a wooden stile. This allows entry onto Abdy golf course.

Over the stile turn sharp right along the path which clings to the perimeter of the course for 100 yards to a waymarker post. By this turn left to stay to the left of a small stream. By the far end of a tiny pond turn right, as shown by another waymarker, onto a maintained path leading towards the former Abdy Farm, now the club house of the golf club.

At the first junction, by the corner of the farm buildings and a footpath sign, turn left into Abdy Lane. At the first junction, and by another footpath sign, turn left, staying along the lane as it passes between luxuriant hedgerows with yellowhammers and pied wagtails flitting about.

Beyond a large metal pylon corner to the right, ignoring all temptations to turn onto a succession of paths leading back into Wath Woods. Remain along the lane until it meets Blackamoor Road. Turn left and, using the verge as a footpath, head back towards the traffic island and the Woodman Inn.

Walk 28. Wentworth

This route around the heart of the Wentworth Woodhouse estate finally passes through the parkland and by the house, reputedly the largest private residence in England.

Route: Wentworth — Street Lane — Hoober Stand — Hoober — Nether Haugh — Hollin Hall — Dog Kennel Pond — Wentworth Woodhouse — Wentworth

Start: The Rockingham Arms, Wentworth. Map reference 388981

Distance: 6 miles.

Maps: 1. "Sheffield (North) & Stocksbridge", number 726 in the Ordnance Survey's "Pathfinder" series. 2. "Rotherham", number 727 in the Ordnance Survey's "Pathfinder" series.

Public Transport: Wentworth is served by frequent daily buses from Rotherham and Barnsley.

By Car: Wentworth stands on the B6090 which links the village of Kilnhurst with Harley which is on the A6135 road between Hoyland Common and Chapeltown. It may also be reached along the B6092 from Swinton and the 6091 from Rawmarsh. There is a large car park in the village close to the Rockingham Arms.

Refreshments: The Rockingham Arms and the George and Dragon both serve bar meals at lunch time and during the evenings. There is also the Blacksmith's Cafe in the village.

The Rockingham Arms

As befits the established meeting place of the Fitzwilliam Hunt, the Rockingham Arms is embellished with hunting horns, hunting maps and hunting prints which adds to the ambience of its role as an estate pub, complete with the Wentworth coat-of-arms.

The emphasis is on the traditional with brassware, pottery, exposed brickwork and stonework, large open fire and thick, exposed wooden beams. Even the old-style settles are redolent with history.

This old coaching inn, which is also residential, offers the hungry walker an extensive and mouth-watering menu of bar meals. Honeydew melons, steak and kidney pie, fresh fish, sirloin steak, lasagne, lentil soup, stuffed marrow and Yorkshire Puddings with a selection of fillings, all complicate the problem of choice. This excellent fare is matched by Younger's Bitter, Younger's No. 3, Theakston's Old Peculier and Theakston's XB, all cask conditioned and on hand pump. If these will not suffice there is a choice of lagers and ciders, not to mention a fine array of malt whiskies and other wines and spirits.

When I was a boy, the Rockingham Arms was officially closed on Sundays because of some licensing peculiarity but you could always enter through the back door for a pint. Today that anomaly has ended and it enjoys normal opening hours.

Opening Times: Mondays to Saturdays, 11.00 a.m. to 3.00 p.m. and 5.30 p.m. to 11.00 p.m.; Sundays, 12.00 a.m. to 3.00 p.m. and 7.00 p.m. to 10.30 p.m.

The Rockingham Arms

Wentworth Woodhouse

With its stone cottages, almshouses and churches, Wentworth bears all the hall marks of a typical estate village and there has been remarkably little modern development. It is controlled by the Rockingham Estate which, in turn, is centred on Wentworth Woodhouse which is reputed to be the largest private residence in England.

For centuries the Wentworth family not only dominated the county of Yorkshire but were also a power in the land. In the twelfth century the Canons of Bolton Abbey, near Skipton, let the estate in South Yorkshire to a family which took the name of Wentworth. They built the first Wentworth Woodhouse and, although the name may have signified a wooden building, it may also mean "The house in the wood"

The family first came to prominence when Thomas Wentworth was appointed chief adviser to King Charles I shortly before the Civil War. Indeed, it was probably the policies he advocated along with those of Archbishop Laud which promoted the crisis and he became one of the most hated men in England with the nickname, "Black Tom Tyrant".

When Parliament gained the upper hand he was brought to trial and, as a result of the verdict which was a forgone conclusion, he lost his head. It is believed that he was buried in the parish church at Hooton Roberts (see Walk 24) and during excavations carried out during the 1890s a headless body was discovered there.

The estate eventually passed to Thomas Watson Wentworth who became Lord Malton in 1728 and 1st Marquess of Rockingham in 1746. His son Charles inherited the title and served two periods as Prime Minister. During the second of these he concluded the peace which allowed the United States independence. He wielded a large amount of political influence and on one occasion spent £21, 000 in buying votes to win a single election in the City of York and this barely touched his personal fortune.

Through his marriage to an heiress of the Bright family the estate was enlarged to cover most of South Yorkshire and included the manor of Eccleshall which included what is now the Abbeydale Industrial Hamlet. It was also involved with the Rockingham Pottery at Swinton (see walk 27).

The title died out with the tenth Earl Fitzwilliam who died without male heirs in 1979. By then the Estate had been sold and the house had become an educational college but, a few years ago, it was bought by a multi- millionaire for his private residence and life in Wentworth goes on much as it has always done.

The house itself is built mainly in the eighteenth century classical style. The West Front was added between 1725 and 1734 being constructed of red brick and sandstone. In 1734 work started on the East Front to a design by Henry Flitcroft and was completed several years later. The 4th Earl of Fitzwilliam employed the celebrated York architect, John Carr, to add a further storey to each wing to provide extra quarters for the servants. Tradition tells of servants actually getting lost as they went from one section of the house to another and it is also reputed to have as many windows as there are days in the year.

There is also an impressive stable block built by the second Marquess of Rockingham. A great patron of horse racing, he was also responsible with some of his friends for building the grandstand on York's Knavesmire racecourse. His stables at Wentworth housed 84 horses and were so large that they included an indoor riding school and coach houses.

Follies

The Wentworth Estate is also renowned for the number of follies built in prominent positions. The most famous is Hoober Stand, a triangular tower which stands more 100 feet high and is some 518 feet above sea level. It was constructed between 1747 and 1749 by the 1st Marquess of Rockingham to celebrate the crushing of the second Jacobite Rebellion in 1746 in which he served under the Duke of Cumberland. It also serves to mark his elevation from Lord Malton to the Marquessate of Rockingham. It cost £300 to build. Until fairly recent times it was open to the public and from the top the view was so extensive it included York Minster, some 40 miles distant. Unfortunately it had to be closed because subsidence in the area through coal mining made the foundations unsafe.

Although not open to the public, the Wentworth Mausoleum stands close to this route and is visible through the trees. It houses a life-size statue of the 2nd Lord Rockingham surrounded by the busts of the members of his cabinet.

Another folly (visited on Walk 29) is the Needle's Eye. This is a tower in the shape of a pyramid which is pierced by a carriageway. According to local tradition it was erected by Lord Rockingham so that he could drive a horse and carriage through it to win a wager that he could drive such a vehicle "through the eye of a needle".

The Route

From the Rockingham Arms turn left along Main Street and at the junction by the War Memorial make a left turn into Cortworth Lane, soon passing the main entrance into Wentworth Woodhouse Park on your right.

Continue along Cortworth Lane to the next road junction. Ignore Coaley Lane which runs off to the left and is signed to Brampton. Instead, fork right, still along Cortworth Lane, in the direction signed to Kilnhurst. However, after 200 yards, turn left into the approach to Cortworth House, indicated as a public footpath by a sign on the opposite side of the road.

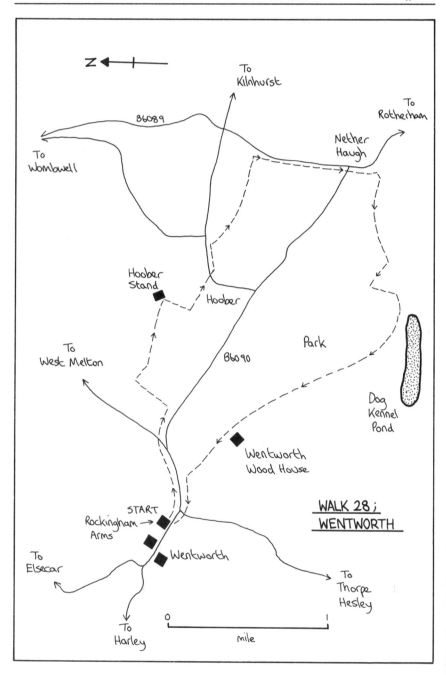

N

To
Kilnhurst

To
Rotherham

B6089

Nether
Haugh

To
Wombwell

Hoober
Stand

Hoober

To
West Melton

Park

B6090

Dog
Kennel
Pond

Wentworth
Wood House

WALK 28;
WENTWORTH

START

Rockingham
Arms

Wentworth

To
Elsecar

To
Thorpe
Hesley

To
Harley

0   1

mile

Where the driveway curves to the left after 100 yards, maintain direction through a waymarked wicket gate, staying to the right of a hedge along the boundary of an arable field. After passing to the right of a red brick house, use the stone step stile adjacent to a gateway to emerge onto the Street, a surfaced lane.

Turn right. Approximately 100 yards beyond a row of stone cottages on your left, and by another footpath post, turn left over a very low stone step stile and then veer towards the right in following a very clear footpath towards some woods while aiming a little to the left of Hoober Stand.

On reaching the corner of a hedge beneath some overhead power lines, make a right turn through 45 degrees. After negotiating the next stile turn left into a clump of trees to a Y-junction after 15 yards. Fork right. The path twists its way through the trees to Hoober Stand which is fenced-off. Stay to the right to reach a lane where a seat is provided. It makes an excellent spot for enjoying a panoramic view over South Yorkshire.

Turn right down the hedged lane, descending gradually to a wooden stile. Beyond this the lane develops into a simple field path. Remain to the left of a hedge to a stone step stile which is but a short distance to the right of a modernised stone house with a footpath sign alongside.

There turn left along Street Lane, at this point unsurfaced and follow it until reaching the B6090 on a bend in the hamlet of Hoober.

Emerging onto the road maintain the same line of direction in the direction of Swinton and Kilnhurst. After 200 yards you will reach a footpath sign opposite a bungalow, "Clematis". Turn right but do not proceed down the obvious drive. Instead, negotiate the stile by the telegraph pole to enter the woods, reaching a second wooden stile after 150 yards.

Leave the woods at this point by maintaining direction along the obvious path which leads over the Roman Ridge and passes under some overhead wires before arriving at another stile. Negotiate this to follow the distinctive path over the field to meet the B6089 at Low Stubbin.

Turn right along this for approximately half a mile into the village of Nether Haugh. A few yards beyond the post box and before a road sign for horses, turn right into Daniel Lane. By the last of the houses go right by a footpath sign into a very narrow lane which soon develops into a field path with a hedge on the right.

In the first field corner turn left and, in the second corner, turn right over a stile before veering left over an open field to the facing hedge. On reaching this, turn left again so that the hedge in on your right. Lose height but, in the bottom of the field, make a right turn over a footbridge which has a waymarked stile at the far end. Over this, turn right. Continue until meeting a broad track closed off to the right by a five-barred metal gate. Hollin Hall is to the right.

Turn left along this lane which follows the course of a Roman ridge and has a row of trees on the left. A short distance before Dog Kennel Pond turn right along another broad path which goes between the Deer Shed and Peacock Lodge to cross the parkland of Wentworth Woodhouse which was landscaped by Humphrey Repton.

After a considerable distance the path stays to the right of the main house with its extensive facade to join a surfaced drive. Follow this as it passes the stable block to leave the park by the main entrance. Turn left along Cortworth Lane and retrace your outward steps to the Rockingham Arms.

Walk 29. Elsecar

A route through a rural oasis which has survived in the heart of the South Yorkshire coalfield thanks to the influence of one of the great landowning families of England. It uses field paths and bridleways to traverse a rolling landscape.

Route: Elsecar – King's Wood – Clay Field – Coley Lane – Lee Wood – Linthwaite – Elsecar

Start: Elsecar Heritage, Elsecar. Map reference 384999.

Distance: 3½ miles.

Map: "Sheffield (North) & Stocksbridge", number 726 in the Ordnance Survey's "Pathfinder" series.

Public Transport: The start is served by frequent daily buses from Barnsley, Rotherham and Sheffield (not Sundays). Elsecar station has direct trains from Sheffield, Huddersfield and Leeds. From the station turn right down Hill Street and continue into Fitzwilliam Street until reaching Elsecar Heritage which stands at the junction of Fitzwilliam Street with Armroyd Lane.

By Car: Elsecar Heritage is signed from the A6135 Chapeltown to Barnsley road at map reference 365988. Follow Broadcarr Road and turn right into Armroyd Lane. There are two large car parks at Elsecar Heritage.

Refreshments: The Milton Arms serves bar meals at lunch time and in the evenings. There is a cafe at the Elsecar Heritage Centre with limited opening hours. A slight diversion leads into Wentworth village where there are two pubs serving bar meals and also the Old Blacksmith's Cafe.

The Milton Arms

The Milton Arms with its cheerful, white exterior decorated with hanging floral baskets in summer, stands at the junction of Armroyd Lane with Fitzwilliam Street, Elsecar, and is only a few yards from Elsecar Heritage.

Its interior atmosphere is more reminiscent of a country pub than one normally found in a mining area. The bar is divided into two areas, both with beamed ceilings, floor tiles, cast iron work and a three-sided mahogany bar. The walls are decorated with pictures of horse-drawn vehicles and canal scenes which is not surprising since it stands close to the former terminus of the Elsecar Branch of the Dearne and Dove

Canal. In addition to the enterprising range of bar food it offers Stones Best Bitter, Bass, Spitfire from Shepherd Neame, John Smith's Best Bitter and Worthington's Best Bitter, all cask conditioned. In addition there are lagers and cider on draught.

Opening Times: Mondays to Saturdays, 12.00 a.m. to 3.00 p.m. and 7.00 p.m. to 11.00 p.m.; Sundays, 12.00 a.m. to 3.00 p.m. and 7.00 p.m. to 10.30 p.m.

Elsecar Heritage Centre

The Route

Exit the car park and turn right along Forge Lane which flanks Elsecar Heritage. By the far corner of the museum there is a Y-junction with a footpath finger post.

Go right along another lane for 40 yards before turning left by a waymarker post and climbing a large field towards a wooden pylon. Stay to the right of this, pass beneath the wires and enter King's Wood, reaching a Y-junction after 20 yards. Fork right, staying just inside the boundary of this mixed broad-leaved woodland and gaining height as the wood pigeon, robins and wrens call.

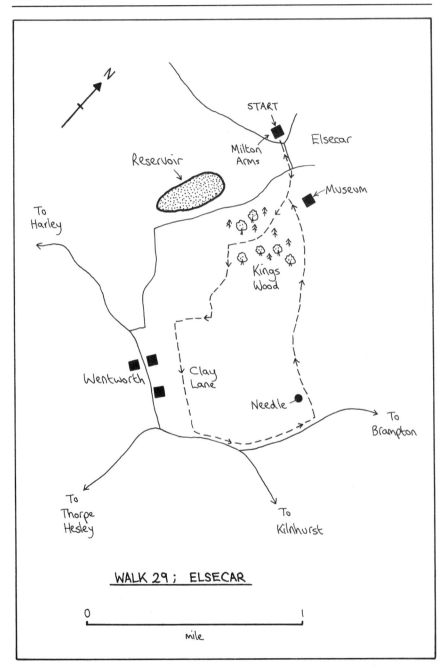

WALK 29 ; ELSECAR

The path is both firm and clear, ultimately levelling and curving left to a wooden stile. Using this to leave the wood veer slightly to the left making for the tall tower of Wentworth church which is clearly visible in the far distance.

On reaching a hedge on the far side of this narrow field, however, turn left to walk towards a footpath finger post in the far corner. Away to the right is a fine view of the Pennine Moors rising above Langsett.

Turn right over the stile by the footpath sign and stay alongside a hedge as the path loses height. Half way down the field, and just before a group of oaks, swing left away from the hedge towards the left-hand field corner.

In the corner, turn sharp left between two hedges for 20 yards before making a right turn into a lane which eventually corners left to a T-junction with a three-armed footpath post. Turn left and immediately corner right along Barrow Fields Lane which is one of those good old fashioned English ones flanked by hedgerows and wild flowers.

After some distance, it loses the hedgerow on the right as it develops into a field path crossing the appropriately named Clay Field where pheasants and magpies vie with each other as they call.

Cross a succession of narrow fields using a series of wooden stiles and with the village of Wentworth just a very short distance away to the right. Having passed to the right of a pylon, negotiate the next stile before passing between a garden fence and a hedge to another stile and crossing a small paddock to a stone step stile by a footpath sign. This provides access to a lane. Turn right to a T-junction after 70 yards. Turn left along Clayfield Lane with its metalled surface and with the village cricket ground on your right.

In succession, you will pass the Wentworth Estate Office and an old brick windmill now converted into a private residence. In summer it is worth pausing a short while to admire its delightful cottage garden.

Clayfield Lane ends opposite the main entrance to Wentworth Woodhouse Park (see Walk 28) by forming a T-junction with Cortworth Lane, the B6090. Turn left but, after 300 yards and at the road junction, fork left into Coaley Lane, the road signposted to Brampton. You will soon pass, on your right, the substantial stone built Cortworth House with its sundial.

Continue with the road beyond Lee Wood on your left and Street Lane, a minor road which branches off to the right. By the far end of Stump Cross Cottage (not to be confused with Stump Cross House) look for a footpath sign. By this, turn left up three steps and pass through a kissing gate onto a well maintained path which runs to the right of a hedge along the side of a large cultivated field. There are extensive views of Hoober Stand and the whole of the Dearne Valley to your right.

By a gate on the left divert a few yards to the Needle's Eye folly for the superb view out over Wentworth to the moors in the far distance. Return to the track and resume walking in your original direction. Lee Wood House is a short distance away below and to the right. About 50 yards beyond the end of Lee Wood negotiate a wooden stile and maintain direction with a row of trees on the left and a fence on the right.

Pass a redundant stile and stay forward along the crest of the ridge for a further 150 yards to a second redundant stile which is followed by a fence on the left and an open field on the right as the path begins to lose height.

The mining villages of Elsecar, Hoyland and Birdwell are spread out in front of you. Pass beneath over head wires to a wooden stile adjacent to a five-barred gate after which the rate of descent quickens appreciably.

Pass to the left of Linthwaite Farm and negotiate another wooden stile before crossing the centre of the next field while veering slightly to the right to pass between two fencing posts, one of wood and one of concrete. Beyond these, veer left down the centre of another arable field to a wooden stile which provides access to an intersection in the path network.

Continue forwards onto a narrow path which threads its tortuous route through a clump of hawthorns before widening into a lane. It continues losing height until it joins the outward route by the corner of the Elsecar Heritage Centre. Retrace your steps to the car park.

Walk 30. Jump

A short route through a former mining area using field paths, roads and a canal towpath.

Route: Elsecar — Jump Valley — Jump — Hemingfield — Elephant and Castle — Dove and Dearne Canal — Elsecar.

Start: The Heritage Centre, "Elsecar at Barnsley", Elsecar. map reference 385998.

Distance: 4 miles.

Maps: 1. "Sheffield (North) & Stocksbridge", number 726 in the Ordnance Survey's "Pathfinder" series. 2. "Barnsley & Penistone", number 715 in the Ordnance Survey's "Pathfinder" series.

Public Transport: The start is served by frequent daily buses from Barnsley and Rotherham. Buses from Sheffield (except Sundays). Elsecar station has direct trains from Sheffield, Huddersfield and Leeds. From the station turn right down Hill Street and continue into Fitzwilliam Street until reaching the Heritage Centre, "Elsecar at Barnsley", which stands at the junction of Fitzwilliam Street with Armroyd Lane.

By Car: The Heritage Centre, "Elsecar At Barnsley", is signed from Junction 36 of the M1 motorway and from the A6135 near Birdwell. From the A6135 follow Broadcarr Road and turn right into Armroyd Lane. There are two large car parks by the Heritage Centre.

Refreshments: The Elephant and Castle serves bar meals at lunch time and in the evenings. There is also a cafe with limited opening hours in the Heritage Centre.

Museums:: "Elsecar at Barnsley". Open seven days a week from 8.30 a.m. to 5.30 p.m. Admission free. Telephone: 01226 740203.

The Elephant and Castle

This was a surprising discovery: a delightful and charming canalside pub which has long outlived the commercial artery which gave it life by adapting to changing circumstances. Originally serving a busy wharf on the Elsecar Branch of the Dearne and Dove Canal, it now caters mainly for locals and those walkers who like to stride out along the recently developed Elsecar Greenway.

Built of local stone, standing slightly below street level, it boasts a cosy rectangular bar complete with wooden beams and a stone fireplace which is now occupied by a gas fire. The copper-topped tables are served by seating around the walls. There is also a smaller room through the bar. Outside there is a beer garden with children's playground and the tables look out over the canal where the locks have been converted into miniature waterfalls.

Landlord Frederick Arthur Smith produces a large selection of bar meals at lunch time and in the evenings. For those in search of liquid refreshment there is a choice between cask conditioned John Smith's Bitter and Magnet. In addition there is the Elsecar Brewery's Barnsley Bitter, a traditionally potent brew. For weaker mortals there is a choice of lagers, wines and spirits.

Opening Times: Mondays to Saturdays, 12.00 a.m. to 3.00 p.m. and 7.00 p.m. to 11.00 p.m.; Sundays, 12.00 p.m. to 3.00 p.m. and 7.00 p.m. to 10.30 p.m.

The Elephant and Castle

Elsecar at Barnsley

The strangely named "Elsecar At Barnsley", the Elsecar Heritage Centre, occupies the site of the former Elsecar Workshops. These were the hub of the industrial activity of the Wentworth Estate covering both the mining and engineering enterprises.

They included a blacksmith's shop, granary, joiner's shop, wagon shop and the Earl Fitzwilliam's private railway station with a line linking into the main railway network.

These have now been bought by Barnsley Metropolitan Borough Council and, at the moment, are in process of restoration. Some are already open to the public including "Elsecar People", an exhibition telling the story of the workshops and of the people of both Elsecar and the Wentworth Estate. There is an outdoor science display, a unique collection of typesetting equipment and a bottle collection.

A number of the former workshops have been opened as business enterprises which include Forge Lane Crafts, the Wentworth Pottery and the Wentworth Tinsmith.

The Powerhouse will re-open as an educational exhibition to provide hands-on experiences involving different types of energy and power. Work is in hand on restoring the Newcomen beam engine and the cottages in Fitzwilliam Square will be restored as typical examples of Victorian working class homes.

Elsecar at Barnsley

The Route

From the Heritage Centre car park cross Forge Lane to enter the museum, "Elsecar At Barnsley". Continue forward keeping the Powerhouse on your right to reach Blacksmith Square. Turn right and Cross Fitzwilliam Square into Darwin Yard. Leave the Heritage Centre by the Darwin Yard entrance and cross Distillery Side to pass through a metal gate.

With the restored railway line on your right and a new brick-built factory on your left, maintain direction across a small area of open ground. As this narrows you draw opposite Elsecar Church with its tall steeple away to your left. By a group of willow trees turn left but, staying to the right of the slipway, take the footpath right of the Elsecar Branch of the Dearne and Dove Canal. It soon enters open countryside with ragwort and buttercups attracting large numbers of white butterflies during the summer months.

Soon the path swings to the right to form a T-junction with the Elsecar Greenway, a new walking route which runs from Elsecar to Wombwell. Turn left along this as the Greenway moves closer to the canal which, at this point, is partially filled-in and overgrown with lush vegetation.

On reaching Wath Road turn left over the bridge but, after 20 yards, turn right by a footpath sign to walk a clear, well-trodden path alongside the boundary hedge on your left. Where this terminates continue across the open field with a set of garden allotments and pigeon lofts on the immediate left. These are a typical reminder that this was, until recently, a thriving mining area.

On reaching an enormous black pipe on the right, swing sharply to the left onto a wide track which passes between two small housing estates before crossing an estate road to enter a wide but unsigned lane which soon starts to climb.

It passes under a railway viaduct and crosses another estate road before meeting Wentworth Road. Turn right along this, climbing steeply round the bend to the left. Soon after passing the Post Office you reach a T-junction opposite the Flying Dutchman pub in the centre of the village of Jump.

Turn right along Cemetery Road. Initially this is lined with stone cottages, the gaps between which afford views of Wentworth Church, Keppel's Column and Hoober Stand. Pass both the cemetery and the War Memorial before crossing over the railway and reaching the Fiddler's Inn on your right. 15 yards beyond this and by a house corner and a footpath sign, turn right onto a path which is cobbled with bricks. These soon give way to an earth surface and there is a fence on your

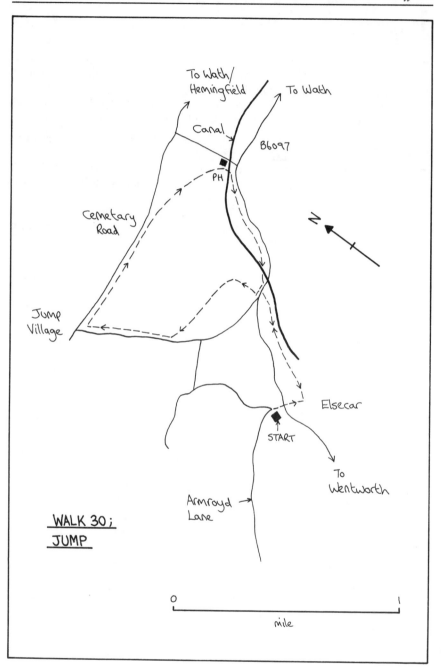

To Wath/
Hemingfield

To Wath

Canal

B6097

PH

Cemetary
Road

N

Jump
Village

Elsecar

START

To
Wentworth

Armroyd
Lane

**WALK 30;
JUMP**

0   1

mile

right and a hedge on your left. Behind the fence are some dilapidated farm huts.

On entering a large arable field turn left along the clear path which stays to the right of a hedge before developing into a lane to pass a cluster of huts to emerge onto Tingle Bridge Lane.

Turn right along this minor road for 20 yards to the Elephant and Castle pub. After refreshments continue towards the canal and, having crossed over Tingle Bridge and by the footpath and Elsecar Greenway sings, turn right along the towpath so that the canal is on your right.

Here it passes through open country with the slope to your right being clothed in trees and large patches of gorse. the former locks have been modified into cascades with mallard, coot and moorhen displaying their presence. It is difficult to imagine that, until a few years ago, this was the scene of heavy industry.

Soon the railway appears on the left and there are glimpses of Jump village away to the right. On reaching Wath Road, cross directly to retrace your steps for the final quarter of a mile to your starting point.

If you wish to shorten this walk you can return from the Elephant and Castle by train on certain days when the enthusiasts have steam up for the two mile journey along this former colliery railway line.

More Books about Yorkshire:

YORKSHIRE: A WALK AROUND MY COUNTY – Tony Whittaker *(£7.95)*

SECRET YORK: WALKS WITHIN THE CITY WALLS – Les Pierce *(£6.95)*

PUB WALKS IN THE YORKSHIRE DALES – Clive Price *(£6.95)*

PUB WALKS ON THE NORTH YORK MOORS & COAST – Stephen Rickerby *(£6.95)*

PUB WALKS IN THE YORKSHIRE WOLDS – Tony Whittaker *(£6.95)*

BEST PUB WALKS IN SOUTH YORKSHIRE – Martin Smith *(£6.95)*

YORKSHIRE DALES WALKING: ON THE LEVEL – Norman Buckley *(£6.95)*

STRANGE SOUTH YORKSHIRE – David Clarke *(£6.95)*

More Walks 'Up North':

THE LAKELAND SUMMITS – Tim Synge *(£7.95)*

100 LAKE DISTRICT HILL WALKS – Gordon Brown *(£7.95)*

LAKELAND ROCKY RAMBLES: Geology beneath your feet – Brian Lynas *(£7.95)*

FULL DAYS ON THE FELLS: Challenging Walks – Adrian Dixon *(£7.95)*

PUB WALKS IN THE LAKE DISTRICT – Neil Coates *(£6.95)*

LAKELAND WALKING, ON THE LEVEL – Norman Buckley *(£6.95)*

STROLLING WITH STEAM : walks along the Keswick Railway – Jan Darrall *(£4.95)*

TEA SHOP WALKS IN THE LAKE DISTRICT – Jean Patefield *(£6.95)*

MOSTLY DOWNHILL: LEISURELY WALKS, LAKE DISTRICT – Alan Pears *(£6.95)*

MOSTLY DOWNHILL IN THE PEAK DISTRICT – Clive Price *(£6.95)*
(two volumes, White Peak & Dark Peak)

FIFTY CLASSIC WALKS IN THE PENNINES – Terry Marsh *(£8.95)*

- plus many more entertaining and educational books being regularly added to our list.
All of our books are available from your local bookshop. In case of difficulty, or to obtain our
complete catalogue, please contact:

Sigma Leisure, 1 South Oak Lane, Wilmslow, Cheshire SK9 6AR
Phone: 01625 – 531035   Fax: 01625 – 536800

ACCESS and VISA orders welcome – call our friendly sales staff or use our 24 hour Answer-
phone service! Most orders are despatched on the day we receive your order – you could
be enjoying our books in just a couple of days. Please add £2 p&p to all orders.